MOE
THE
WOOLY
MAMMOTH

MOE
THE
WOOLY
MAMMOTH

JENNY SCHREIBER

Meet Moe the woolly mammoth. He is a large, furry animal.

About the Author

Kendall B. Helmly was born and raised in a middle-income suburban setting. Dad was a university STEM professor. Mom was a housewife. One car and one dog growing up in a neighborhood with many children to share aspirations with. Later in life, the desire to write became an obsession. Starting as an amateur poet and graduating to fiction writing, Kendall expresses both the grit and passion of the human experience through storytelling.

"Words have power, good and bad. One's psyche is influenced by their interpretation. Through literature, we experience a silent world of idioms, and freedom of choice reveals our version of the truth."

Dedicated to family, wherever they may be.

Contents

Chapter 1: Mom's a Whore, Dad's a Pimp

I'm sad because my momma doesn't love me. My daddy's gone. Just gone, no goodbye. He went out for cigarettes one day and never came back. Momma wept into a frenzy, clinging to a checkbook with a ten-dollar balance. She yelled in a very hurtful voice, "We don't have food or rent money. It's your fault, you little shit. I got knocked up and carried you around inside me for almost ten months when I was sixteen. Now were abandoned eight years later."

I quipped, "That would make you twenty-four now. Is that right?" Mom reluctantly agreed in a condescending voice, "Yeah, you little smart ass. You are eight and better at math than I am. That's so fucked up. Ronnie, your piece of shit father wanted me to abort you when I got pregnant, but I couldn't do it. Now, I'm very soon to be homeless, and you are going to be put into foster care for your own good."

That was a lot for a third-grader to comprehend all at once. Mom had no filter most of the time. It's lucky my entire vocabulary doesn't completely consist of obscenities. I said shit out loud once in the orphanage and got popped in the mouth for it. Lesson learned. Do your swearing away from grownups. The orphanage I got thrown into sucked. Older kids bullied me, and the adults treated me like dirt. I was nothing but a meal ticket to them. My entire net worth to that point was crammed into an oversized backpack. I looked ridiculous dragging it around. The orphanage they took me to looked more like a prison. Something right out of some B horror movie. I shared a room with three other boys. Our ages were only six months apart. Billy, who had the same first name as me, Jimmy, and Bartholomew. Bart, for short. We got along pretty well. None of us cried ourselves to sleep or wet the bed. We were lucky. In the first-grade room, both boys wet the bed constantly. The smell was awful sometimes. They couldn't help it, though. Small bladders. Mrs. Dirk ran the place, and she was the cook, too. The food was healthy but not long on taste. Salt and pepper shakers would have helped, but none were ever to be found. There was a playground in the backyard. That's where I and my three roommates would hang out most of the time. Everyone would get extremely excited on visitation days. That was when prospective parents would come and look us over. Most of the kids would fall all over each other to get picked for adoption or foster care. I already had parents, and that pretty much ruined any hopes that I had for adoption. My parents were a couple of real losers. They didn't want me around.

After about a year, my so-called, dutiful parents relinquished custody of me to the state. That meant I was now eligible for full adoption. Big deal. I had heard nightmares about foster parents from kids who were brought back to the orphanage due to incompatibility issues. Most didn't even want to talk about it. One little girl named Penelope was adopted by a child molester. She didn't say a word to anyone for over six months. Finally, some friends got her to speak again.

She went to see a special counselor for a long time. Penny, that's what we called her, loved to play on the swings. The far-right swing was hers for the rest of the time she was there. I didn't quite understand what had happened to her, but I knew it wasn't good. Every week, Penelope would go and see Ms. Miranda, who was an art therapist. It took some time before she started to trust anyone again. Most of the older kids had at least heard the term pedophile before. Mrs. Dirk kept her close to the vest for a while after that.

I had no best friend. All my bunkmates liked to do was tell lies about themselves or their dads. Most of the boys claimed their dad was an astronaut. Bart put a spin on that. He said his old man was head of mission control in Houston. When we got bored with that, we would take turns peeking through the window of the girl's shower. It was an anatomy lesson. Once, we saw Mrs. Dirk naked. That was scary; I had already seen Marie naked with a bunch of guys multiple times. Mrs. Dirk was not into health and fitness at all. Plus, she was in her sixties. Billy would tell us wild stories about his dad being a big game hunter, living over in Africa. He would say, I have pictures of him killing a lion and a tiger, but he could never produce them for us to see. I guess he didn't know tigers live in Asia, not Africa. It didn't matter anyway. The stories helped pass the time, and that's something we had plenty of.

Every day after school, we would get off the bus, go straight to the dining hall, have milk and our snack, usually shortbread cookies, and do our homework. When everyone was done, we all got to go outside and play until dinner. We were allowed to help each other. That made it go much faster. On really hot or rainy days, we would stay inside and play games or do coloring books. Individual chores were done before breakfast and after the evening meal, very much like basic training. The chores rotated every month. I liked working in the kitchen, even though it was a lot of work. We had to scrub all the dishes and prep for the next day's meal. There was no TV to watch, so after our chores were done, we had a little free time before bed. Lights out for me, was at 8:30 sharp. The kids twelve and older could stay up until 10 pm. I think the most important thing we got out of the orphanage was structure. Everyone came from a broken, dysfunctional home, with very little accountability or too much in some cases. Once I got used to it, the chores and homework weren't so bad.

At school, everything was different. Mrs. Wilkes, my favorite teacher and an orphan herself, knew exactly how cruel and disillusioned adolescence could be. She was my best friend and mentor all the way up through high school. Because of her kindness, I was the brightest kid in her class. She got me ready for the transition to Junior High School. It seemed newness and shyness sort of ran together for me. Girls ignored me. I was so invisible to them. I was still a social outcast due to my circumstances. I was one of the rejects from the orphanage with no mom or dad. I had both, but that didn't matter to them. The boys in my class would constantly size me up for a fight. Billy Hawks was the most persistent. We got into it every day at recess. To be honest, I think we started to grow on each other. I was smarter, but we were physically equal to each other. Mostly, we just traded insults until the bell rang.

I finally managed to get out of the orphanage and move in with my foster parents. Brad and Betty King agreed to raise me. I was really nervous, having heard such vicious horror stories about foster guardians. I didn't know what to expect. We all got to their house and sat down on the couch in the living room. Brad told me that we were going to take it day by day. For the first few months I would have very little time to myself. I would almost always be chaperoned. That's exactly what happened. It started out fairly similar to the orphanage. Chores in the morning and afternoon, and homework after school. Over time, I actually got to start doing things on my own. Brad was still very strict when it came to doing chores, but I was sort of used to that already. My foster father invented the term tough love. He could be very curt and demanding at times. Mostly fair, though. Brad expected me to pull my own weight around the house. Betty, my foster mom was ok for the most part. She was very loving and supportive at times. Her raisin peanut butter cookies were delicious. She would make a batch up on most Wednesdays. I ran home from school a lot on Wed.

Brad and Betty really liked having sex. They did it constantly, at least three to four times a week. That's just the times I knew about. They really seemed to enjoy each other, and both of them were notably easier to get along with right after tearing one-off. I think the term to describe them was horny toads. Sometimes, it could get very colorful around the house. Neither one drank much, at least not around me. They would share a bottle of spirits to celebrate the holidays, but that was about it. Brad was always encouraging me not to get mixed up with any vices. Gambling, smoking, drugs, alcohol, and sexual addiction were very avoidable mistakes. He said that kind of stuff almost always led to a perverted sense of reality. It would hurt me in the long run.

Brad was no Saint! He was a wild hellion in his youth. He mostly played baseball growing up. He was so good that several pro scouts were interested, including the Yankees and Dodgers. But unfortunately, he blew his knee out sliding into second base, during a state playoff game his senior year in high school.

Boy, did he love baseball. One Saturday, we went to see the Houston Astros play the Atlanta Braves. I forgot to mention we lived in Galveston, Texas.

Before the game, we got hot dogs and cracker jacks. I will never forget that day. I learned more about Brad in eight hours than in the eighteen months I had been fostered by him and Betty. He grew up in Fort Riley, Kansas. His old man was a Sergeant Major in the Army there. Brad was an Army brat. He was lucky, though. His dad lost a leg in Korea, so they didn't have to travel around much. Brad was a standout athlete in high school. In his senior year, he broke the state high school home run, stolen base, RBI, and batting average record. His dreams were shattered along with his knee during the state semifinals. Without Brad's bat in the lineup, the Fort Riley Wildcats lost the championship six to three. That brought on a lengthy bought of depression for him. He ended up graduating high school from the hospital, healing from his broken leg.

At the game, we got to watch his all-time favorite player, Hank Aaron, go three for four with a three-run homer in the 5th inning. That ball screamed all the way to the center field stands. Brad started to cry when Aaron hit that home run. As he wiped the tears from his eyes, he told me that was a dream of his ever since he was in little league. He said, "I always wanted to see the Hammer hit a home run live in person." Brad told me Aaron was one of only five men to have short careers in the Negro Baseball League and be voted into the National Baseball Hall of Fame by the Sports Writers. The other four are Jackie Robinson, Willie Mays, Roy Campanella, and Ernie Banks. Aaron also had over 3000 hits, and is first on the lifetime RBI list. He also told me those five players endured a ton of racist sentiment most of their outstanding careers.

I will never forget that game. The smells, the food, and the conversation will be etched in my mind until my last days on earth. For the first time in my relationship with Brad, I really understood where he was coming from. It must have been frantically disappointing to lose all of one's hopes and dreams in one instant. I'm convinced that he felt like dying after the shock of the injury wore off. He was just eighteen and on the cusp of greatness. How many sleepless nights did he spend daydreaming of a career in the Majors. It just was not to be. I got to see his most prized possession once, a Jimmy Foxx baseball card. After I saw it, he put it back in his safe. I can't guess what that card is worth now. Baseball was definitely Brad's first love, but Betty owned his heart.

I don't know exactly when Brad met Betty, but they must have been stupid bat crazy for one another. They've been married six years and still carry on like newlyweds. Sadly, they tried to have children of their own but couldn't. That motivated them to enlist as foster caregivers. I was grateful they did, well, most of the time. The exception was when they were getting on to me about chores and homework. They were fair. I never got punished for anything I didn't deserve; Brad only spanked me once when I was nine. I decided to do number two in the backyard, poured lighter fluid on it, and set the turd on fire to get rid of the evidence. That's the last time I take any advice from Billy Hawks. They both came running outside. Brad doused the flame with a big bucket of water. They both dragged me into the house, kicking and screaming. Then, I got a ten-minute lecture on fire safety. Then Brad gave me a spanking.

After that, another fifteen-minute lecture, and I was grounded for a week. Tough love, alright.

That set me straight pretty much for the rest of my adolescence. That was the first time I heard the words, (everything is not all about you.) For my biological mother, Marie, it was always all about her. Good or bad, she came first, unless Ronnie was around, then it was different because the entire universe revolved around him. He was Mister Vice. Drinking, smoking, gambling, dealing drugs, sexual addiction, etc. The man was into pleasure in a big way. With the exception of drug dealing, the man never did a day's work in his life. As a young kid, I picked up on these things. I thought it was the norm. Didn't everyone sell drugs for a living. I went to the pharmacy with Betty to pick up her prescription. After we passed through the drive-up window, I asked her how many of those she was going to sell. She was shocked, then thought for a minute, and asked me, "Did your mom sell her prescriptions?" I said, "Yeah, and mine, too." She just hugged me and told me I would never have to worry about that ever happening again. My social worker, Emily, asked me about that at our next session. At first, I didn't like going to see Miss Emily, but over time, I liked the fact that I could tell her anything. Even the awkward sex questions she was cool with. I asked how oral sex worked. She giggled a little at first. I guess she didn't expect an eleven-year-old to be so blunt. Then I came clean about Marie and all of the men she had been with and how I could hear her getting smacked around by up to three guys at a time, penetrating her every orifice. I would sometimes peek under the window shade from outside. It was confusing for me at the age of eight to watch how my mom made a living.

Afterward, she would take a long combination shower/bath. Then, chain smokes half a pack of cigarettes. She did what she had to do to stay alive. Emily explained to me that many people use sex for money, power, personal satisfaction, etc., with no regard for their partner, male or female. It is a perversion. She said there was nothing wrong with sex. When it's consensual between loving partners. I inverted, "Like Brad and Betty." She continued, yes, they are very much in love and have great affection for one another. I added, "Boy, do they ever."

Thirteen was awkward for me. I clung tightly to my relationship with Dad. I slipped up one day and called Brad Dad to his face. What did you just call me? I called you Dad. We embraced for several minutes. I quipped; there sure is a lot of pollen in the air today. My eyes are watering. Mine to. It's really bad outside. From that day forward, Betty was Mom, and Brad was Dad. It was official a year later when I was formally adopted; to that point, the happiest day in my life. We were officially and forever three.

Chapter 2: Keith

Junior high was a test of nerves. I had to contend with bullies for the first time. Then I met Keith. He was a defensive tackle on the JV football squad. Nobody gave him any problems at all. He would have played on the varsity team but for his grades. I was able to help him with that. I guess I was his tutor. We spent lots of time at the library. That's where he met Wendy. I would chaperone her to all of Keith's games. I was very happy for Keith that he found a love interest. There was no love triangle between us. Wendy and Keith were a solid couple, end of discussion. I was happy for them, and anyone could see in a moment that they genuinely cared a great deal for each other. I was a little jealous that I didn't have a girlfriend yet. Wendy fixed me up with her friend Diane, but we really didn't hit it off. All she wanted to talk about was softball and basketball. She was on both of the girl's JV squads. She was very smart and very pretty, but just didn't have time for me. We did go to the Junior Prom together. We shared our first French kiss that night. That was exciting. She asked me if I had ever been kissed before. I said no. Then she planted one on me right in the middle of the dancefloor. Puppy love. We saw a bit of each other during the summer, but when we got to High School, she went bonkers over this Varsity tennis player. That ended that.

Ms. Wilkes transferred to my high school. There she was, my Algebra I and Algebra II teacher. I was so lucky. I really excelled at math. She wanted me to join the Math club, but I really was not interested. After high school, we became very good friends. There was a little loose talk that we were romantically involved. The only time I ever kissed her was under the mistletoe at a Christmas party. I used to go and spend an hour or two with her on sunny Sunday afternoons. We talked about everything. I learned her husband died over in Iraq. He was a captain in the Marines. She was twenty-three years older than me, and I already had enough mommy issues. Tess, as I called her, would go on to win teacher of the year, become head of our county school board, and serve in the Texas legislature. She was a great politician with the uncanny ability to get projects done. People liked helping her. There was a lot of LBJ in her; he was a teacher, too. I never mentioned it, but I always thought of Tess as a surrogate mother. I cherished her friendship until the day she died.

I had two good moms and one bad one. My biological mother, Marie, brought me into the world and gave me life. I have to thank her for that. I don't remember much of our relationship while she was with Ronnie. He was always angry about something. Surprisingly, he didn't hit Marie or me very much, or hardly at all. I'm guessing he was beaten as a child. He yelled really loud, though. He was very demanding sexually. I didn't understand a lot of what was going on between them, but it was very vocal, and Marie was always really shaken up about it afterward. Ronnie would take off. Marie would just shut down and do nothing for long periods of time. I would ask her a question, and she would nod her head and just stare off into space. Mentally, she just disappeared from her conscious self. I didn't understand. All I wanted was a mother to keep me occupied for a little while. Ronnie scarred her emotions very deeply. I was lucky. My youth somehow shielded me from contemplating fully what exactly went on between them. I was fortunate to have a social worker who really cared about my welfare. Mr. Hicks specialized in adolescent therapy. I worked through many issues. My emotional scars never really penetrated the surface. Only the reflection of a dutiful child remained, wanting to be free from those confusing memories. Bob Hicks was my poison dart penetrating the heart of the beast.

I don't think Marie was ever truly happy. She was always looking for an escape from her station in life. It isn't that she wanted to be punished by her surroundings, but the consequences of the reckless decisions she made always managed to catch up to her. I didn't help her much. Forcing teenage motherhood on anyone is never beneficial for the parent or the child. She just could not bring herself to abort me. I don't think her life would have turned out much differently if she had gotten an abortion. Ronnie was no help at all. My maternal grandparents tried to be supportive. They gave her a place to stay until I was about four. Marie sabotaged that relationship with all the whoring around and drug use. Finally, my grandparents had enough. They wanted to adopt me and raise me, but Marie would have none of it. Marie and I just took off with Ronnie one early morning and never came back. I don't remember much of Grammie and Gramps. They did love me, though. Their house always smelled really good. Grammie was the best cook. Gramps could make almost anything out of wood, from toys to furniture. He was a real, genuine craftsman. Every stick of furniture in their house was built by him. My grandparents would not condone Marie's counterculture lifestyle. Different ideologies, for sure.

Marie wasn't really into hard drugs, just pot. I think somewhere in that misguided brain of hers was some semblance of a conscience. She should have made a better career choice, though. Letting Ronnie pimp her out almost every night really screwed her up, big time. Sometimes, it was two or three guys at the same time. Supposedly, they filmed a lot of her tricks. Ronnie was evil, but he did let Mom keep half the money. Despite my surroundings she did keep me clothed and fed properly. I was never really cold or hungry. That must have been her maternal instinct coming out. Marijuana was definitely her drug of choice. It was her way of escaping many years after we parted ways. I started receiving correspondence from her. I never responded to any of her letters, though I probably should have. I just couldn't deal with the life she had chosen for herself. The constant barrage of sex, drugs, and Ronnie, of course, was much more than I could handle at the time. Not that I was much better at the age of twenty-one, but at least I was smart enough to know that I was not going to find any of life's difficult answers inside a bag of weed. There's no fortunate wisdom in that.

I forgot to consider how big of a step it was for Marie to reach out like that. Now, I look back and comprehend that I was just being selfish. I didn't know how to feel about Marie. She was my mother, for God's sake, but she had no sense of self-worth. I couldn't find any way to get past the disdain I held for her. I could only thank her for giving me life. I know she quit on herself at a very young age. It couldn't have been easy having a kid when she was still in high school herself. Having all that responsibility thrust upon your person before fully mature adulthood has to put an enormous strain on one's esteem. To wake up one morning and have this incomplete, fragile little person dependent upon you for their very survival would totally freak me out, too. Lucky for her, she had her folks to do some of the child rearing. Eventually the constant intervention by Grandma got to Marie. She just got completely fed up with all the wet nursing and lectures about going back to school and finishing her education. Marie thought she had it sort of figured out, working part-time at a convenience store and turning tricks at night. Almost every night, she would come home smelling of booze and whatever cologne her John's were wearing while they were on top of her. It took lots of hot showers and menthols to get her through the night. I guess it was inevitable that she would die so young of lung cancer. I can't recall a time I didn't see her without a cigarette dangling off her lip. Forty-two years and 19 days after she was born, she was no longer on this earth. My maternal grandparents were in their late thirties when Marie was born. Grandma told me she was an accidental blessing to them that turned nightmarish. The day Ronnie showed up in their lives, everything just went to shit. He was rude, brash, and curt with everyone. Marie was nothing but a good piece of ass to him. I know this because I heard him say it many times. He told all his drinking buddies, and they paid him for their time with her. That's what hurt the most was having to listen to those men get off and just toss her aside when they were through. It gave me such mixed feelings about sex as a prepubescent child. If it hadn't been for Keith and Wendy, I would have probably been a virgin until I was in my late twenties. Keith was everything Ronnie was not. He was patient, respectful, and, most of all, gentle. Seeing them together restored my faith in humanity. I guess it was inevitable they would get married. I was so honored to be the best man at their wedding. That day was such an escape for me. No abuse, no drama, just happiness everywhere.

Marie and Ronnie always seemed to make absolutely deplorable decisions together. For the time being, Ronnie got Mom to make a porn film with two of his friends. Marie ended up getting the Clapp from one or both of those guys. Ronnie sold it to some film producer for $800.00. No royalties and a venereal disease to boot. That was my dad, zero business sense. I guess he knew where his dope was coming from for the next few days. Mom was always having to trade sex with Ronnie for food money. No wonder my comprehension of sex was so warped. There were lots of times I wished Ronnie was dead. He always had this thing he would say to Mom right after he was done having sex with her. He'd say, "That was ok, babe, but if you want any more money, you better put some ass into it." What a dirtbag. Then he would greet me out the door and say, so long, shithead. Ok, dad. I didn't know any better. I think to him, that was a term of endearment. Then, Mom would cry and chain smoke while crashing for the night.

I never understood where the hate and cruelty came from. The disassociation from empathy seemed like a tool one would use to stay dead inside. No emotional excerpts to account for. Just push on and take advantage of every situation, always the alpha. Win! Let the losers expend all that energy trying to cope with why they lose. That's all well and good, but what happens when the alpha is eaten by another alpha? They fall harder and faster than any degree of self-esteem can save them. Then, the self-medicating begins: alcohol, opioids, barbiturates, etc. The elixir of broken esteem can't be found in a bottle. Ronnie was too stubborn or ashamed to admit it was his station in life that was killing him, not the people he was in competition with.

Having Ronnie as a role model made me very shy around girls in high school. I didn't know what to say or how to say it, and usually, I loused it up pretty well. Mom had a hand messing up my understanding of a healthy relationship with girls by her constant promiscuity. I knew women had to be more than just objects of sexual desire, but no one explained how to go about really talking to women, or should I say, listening to women. I didn't learn until much later in life that listening is the key to everything. Money, sex, power, you name it. Learn from the mistakes of others, and you will not share their misfortunes. It was not easy to do because I did good in school. I thought I knew what I was talking about. Not very often, that was the case. People said of me, oh! They know it all and are at it again. Overconfidence will make a man step on his dick in broad daylight, witnessed by God and everyone within ear shy. Again, I didn't know it was not about me. It is very hard to comprehend the wisdom of others at a very young age, especially relationship advice. All those raging hormones telling you that all the backed-up semen in your lower body will soon escape like a giant volcanic eruption. Tough for a horny teenager to get past that. The wet dreams and accidental boners didn't help at all. Thank God we get dick control at twenty-three.

I met my first real girlfriend, Lena, as a senior in high school. I was eighteen and extremely naïve emotionally. She had an alluring Italian accent, dark hair, and dark piercing eyes, and she was not a virgin. The first time I was so nervous, I dropped two condoms on the floor. The first few times, I had to wear three condoms to desensitize me. She could make me cum so much. Lena was amazing in bed. She told me not to get hung up on her because she would only break my heart in the end. Despite her warning, she will always have a small place in my heart. Man, sometimes I thought the bedsheets were going to crawl right up my ass when she was on top of me. No cuddling after. Cuddling was for lovers, not friends with benefits. She humped my brains out for four months, then moved on. Lena wasn't big on pomp and circumstance. Thursday nights, it was burgers, shakes, and great sex.

We were in a diner waiting to be served when one of her old boyfriends showed up and started razzing me up and down. Lena told him I only had to wear one condom, and he had to wear four to keep from coming so fast, and sometimes that didn't even work. Tony, that is what she called him, was really pissed. He and his friends waited outside for us to leave. They dragged us down an alley, and Tony pulled out a blade. So, I pulled out a blade and tossed it right into his left thigh. We scampered off while he proceeded to whine like a baby. That was the end of that fight. Poor guy got himself shot in a gang fight about a year later. Anyway, after the fight, we went back to her place, and she made the sheets crawl up my ass again. Lena was four years older than me. She taught me how to be sexually pleasing to a woman. For that, I was eternally grateful. For the first time, I felt that I had value in a relationship with a woman. We talked quite a bit about life in general. Lena was no philosopher, but she had a great deal of common sense at the age of twenty-two. My life was so much richer having known her those four months. When she went back to grad school in the fall. I felt no remorse or disappointment. Instead,

I had found value in myself. I still didn't really know when to keep my big mouth shut. Unfortunately, that would come much later. I would not develop reliable social filters until my thirties, pretty much like most guys. Men in their late teens and early twenties just don't realize the damage that words can do in some situations. It may not be intentional, but the potential for great harm is there. Say something out of turn that impacts another and the damage is done. Words have the capacity to help and harm with the same amount of force. I never realized this until I became skilled at active listening. I learned to not only look at where the words were coming from but also tone, text, and body language, which could be as telling as the words. A good listener has to not only hear spoken words but taste them as well. Also, one must always consider the source very carefully. Always!

I would not retain active listening as a skill until I started to seek out a mental counselor after my enlistment in the U. S. Army. It wasn't until then that I realized just how scary the relationship between Marie and Ronnie was to my psyche. I struggled with anger management, stress management, abandonment, depression, and probably PTSD. Therapy saved many of my relationships. I would soon have to call upon those newfound coping skills to survive September 11th, 2001.

The Army taught me many things. Mostly, how to get along with my superiors. If a soldier can't follow orders, then they are useless. Several of my cohorts ended up washing out within the first two years. After that, all the wannabes were gone. The commanders in West Germany didn't have time to waste on soldiers who couldn't get the job done. The Cold War was coming to a close. It was a very transitional time for the armed forces in Europe. I mustered out a few months before the Berlin Wall came down. Eisenhower was right; all we had to do to defeat communism was wait until the USSR imploded from within. Russia's form of communism was doomed from the start. There were too many people to control. A grassroots movement demanding more civil liberties was inevitable. It finally came in 1991.

I did end up working my ass off in Germany for eighteen months. Honestly, I needed it. Lesson one was, absolutely, nothing I took part in was all about me. That ship sailed out of my head even earlier, during my first day in basic training. For the first sixteen weeks in the service, I was under the direct supervision of three Drill sergeants. Mean as snakes, they were, and twice as dangerous. They did not tolerate any nonconformity. I managed to get through with most of my dignity intact. I failed one exam the entire time I was in basic. I got it right the second time. Good thing because if I had failed any portion of the training three times, I would have been sent home with no questions asked. It would have been like I was never there. After fifteen weeks of nothing but "yes, Drill Sergeant," there was no way I wasn't passing my final tests.

Basic was done. Now, it was off to my permanent duty station. More superior officers telling me exactly what to do and when to do it. I'm thinking to myself, when does it get easier. Eventually, it did, but not until I took quite a few lumps along the way. Germany was the prize. My cohorts and I really got to enjoy the time we had off duty. The German people were amazing; most of them really liked the fact that we were there as part of the NATO forces. We had to try and forget the fact that if the Soviets ever decided to invade, all 300,000 of us were to die in place, buying time for the main force to arrive from the U. S. and relieve what was left after the initial Soviet wave hit. You learn to get used to it. The situation could have been worse. I could have been sent to Korea. The demilitarized zone over there was a true war zone. When they went on full alert, it meant go time. The troops stationed there were the real pawns in the Cold War chess game with the Russians.

Getting back to American soil after it was all over felt incredible. I learned not to take anything for granted. I didn't go through what the servicemen coming home from Vietnam faced by any means; technically, the US was in a peacetime buildup. No fancy parades welcoming me home, but no protesters either. When I was released from active duty, I mustered out with almost $4000.00 in my pocket. A very nice little nest egg. Now, what do I do?

I kind of bounced around the Texas panhandle for a little while. I worked odd jobs, mostly as an auto mechanic. The economy was pretty good at that time, and I still had most of my savings left. My bestie from high school. Keith was a professional firefighter in NYC and on duty when the planes deliberately flew into the Twin Towers. He was on one of the lower floors when Tower One collapsed on top of him. He probably died instantly or close to it. He and Wendy were married then and had been for some time. Keith's death hit me very hard; I immediately went back to the Army. I was really pissed off over 9-11. I really wanted to put my boots on the ground and kill some Al-Kaieda.

Turned out that my Army test scores were extremely good, so I spent my next enlistment working for Army intelligence in

Virginia. All I really did was decode messages and hand them off to someone else to interpret. It paid the bills, and I really felt part of something. It didn't completely make up for the loss of Keith, but it definitely helped. The recruiter made my job in the army sound so cloak and dagger. But it was very nine to five. I did like cleaning out all the MPs at poker. Their tells were so obvious it was like hooking fish in a barrel. The only useful life skill Ronnie ever taught me was poker. He was very good at it. It probably got him killed in Vegas. Supposedly, he conned his way into a braced game in one of the casinos and got caught cheating. His body was certainly given a vulture's funeral somewhere in the Nevada desert.

As my enlistment was coming to an end my commanding officer offered to recommend me for Officer's Candidate School. I respectfully declined. I enjoyed my time in the service, but no way did I want to make it a career. Too much stress for too little reward. Some guys I served with really ate that shit up. The head rush of being wired into everything all at once. It was the lack of positive control I could not get my head around. No amount of intelligence could guarantee that your platoon wouldn't be completely wiped out on the very next mission. For me, I need due process. The Army doesn't work that way.

Maybe it is just a coin flip whether we live or die each passing day. I decide to take a cab to work one morning, and the bus I normally ride gets hit by a train. I know human life is very fragile. As much as we think so, we don't have that much impact on our surroundings. I wake up in the morning and travel along the parameters guiding me through the day. Occasionally, I get to decide something on my own, what to wear, eat, how to get to work, etc. The big decisions have already been made for me. Is today much like any other, or is this Armageddon? Certainly, 9-11 felt that way. I miss Keith. He was a good friend, maybe my only true-blue friend. Only time will bear the knowledge of that. The kind of friend who would bring you soup when you were sick. I'm sure Wendy did. Keith was the kind of person your mother wanted you to be. We've all heard it, why can't you be like so and so, they call their mother all the time. They won't let a little old lady fend for herself in these horrid times. Mashers and muggers everywhere taking advantage of an old woman, who is still very desirable, by the way, left to fend for herself with nothing but an old hound dog and an iron skillet for protection. Shame on you, son. Now, have a nice day, and say hello to the wife and kids for me. It has been ages since you have called or come around for a visit. Please call first; I may be entertaining a gentleman caller.

So, most moms are fickle; that's not a shock by any means. Don't get me wrong, I love my friend's grandmothers to death, but man, they could lay a guilt trip on them as big as a semi-tractor trailer. They would start with, you should call more often. I don't know how much longer I will be around. I would hate for you to have to live with all that guilt for not calling me on my deathbed.

Marie and Ronnie were not the homebody type. What little I remember of Marie's parents faded away quickly; so much pain and drama. Betty and Brad had already buried their parents before I met them. I wish I had. Grandparents are a window into the past. It's not the oodles of cool stuff they have accumulated over the years but the stories about how they lived before all this technology started to take over every facet of modern life. Kids today can't write in cursive or read a non-digital clock. Tell them it's quarter to five, and they will complain they don't have any change in their pocket. They can't use a tape measure, either. Isn't modern technology wonderful. A serious power grid loss in the US could cripple our economy and cause massive food riots and looting on every street corner. I shudder just thinking about it. Thank God I have had extensive firearms training. Break into my apartment, and you will be greeted with a big 44 magnum.

Chapter 3: Too Many Losses

Family aside, I miss Keith. He probably would have been a standout athlete in college, maybe even made the pros, but he was too selfless for that. We were sitting in his backyard one quiet Sunday afternoon, and he said, Billy, God made me 6' 10", 275 lbs. for a reason. Not for gridiron glory but to save lives. With God's help I am going to keep as many people as I can out of harm's way. Fire is hell on earth! No one deserves to die that way, and I'm going to do everything I can to see that it doesn't happen on my watch. Talk about a life of (not about me!) I think he was born to be a firefighter. While giving his eulogy, I told everyone Keith had rescued more than a hundred stranded victims from burning structures in his short career as a firefighter. He was a man who inspired others to go beyond normal expectations. Keith was a silent, gracious hero all of his days on Earth. I was blessed to call him my friend.

After the memorial service ended, one of the church deacons was very complimentary of my words. He told me that was one of the best eulogies he had ever heard, and my words were lovely. He went on to say, "Son, have you ever considered becoming a clergyman? You would make a fine preacher someday." He liked hearing my words and that I put people's minds at ease on such a solemn occasion.

I thought quite a bit about what the old man told me. I have fairly good leadership skills. I am no saint; who is? Can I presume to consider giving myself to a life of service? Given all the demons my real parents thrust upon me in my adolescence, could I be trusted to do God's work? I have never felt God's hand upon me. However, there was one time I was walking home from school, and the front doors to the Methodist church were wide open. I walked in. The place was empty. I walked up to the altar and sat down on the steps. I felt very relaxed, almost like I was sitting in my room. There was something very familiar about my surroundings. I gazed up at the stained-glass icons. Some I recognized, some I did not. It was like having déjà vu. A man walked into the sanctuary and said welcome to God's house, son. I figured he was a preacher. He asked me why I stopped by, and I told him I was walking by, and the doors were wide open. It was like something called out to me to walk inside. A faint whisper disguised as a gust of wind. He said that was odd because he had just closed them a few minutes ago to avoid the rain. That's when I started to get weirded out and took off for home. Very soon after that, Brad and I started spending more time with each other. We started going to baseball games together. I began to consider for a moment that maybe God had planned a life of service for me. I did know one thing for sure, I would be a clergyman who could have a wife and family to love and cherish. Surely, most people would assume if I enrolled in divinity school, I did it out of some loyalty to Keith. That was just the last piece, not the entire puzzle. That, combined with the eulogy, convinced me that I should enroll in divinity school. I just kept telling myself it's not about me. It's never been about me. There is so much hurt and burden in the world; it's time to pitch in. If I can convince just one other person to forgive and give of themselves, then they might follow suite. Life is hard enough. We all have to give back something if there is any truth to the concept of karma. I do believe that we all reap what we sow.

I soon learned that Divinity school was more about convincing other people to recognize God's presence than myself. Still, there are many rewarding benefits associated with living a life of faith and forgiveness. The Bible presents a multitude of reasons and examples for living a moral and nonviolent lifestyle. A moral lifestyle tends to be less expensive. No vices to pay for. While on earth, we are God's flock. It is our duty to protect the earth as much as possible. I don't think God wanted humans to put so much emphasis on consumerism. We have an entire industry dedicated to removing and disposing of our unwanted goods. Only a small percentage can be completely recycled. Somehow, I don't think people really need all of the post-consumer luxury items that we all deem necessary for sustaining a tolerable quality of life. Stop making so much junk. I know, let's outlaw plastic. Wouldn't that be a scary concept? No more plastic water bottles, soda bottles, shrink wrap, cellophane, etc. people don't need an entire closet full of clothing and shoes. Next time, rent your formal attire. Greed has perverted our sensibility to moderate living. I must have this. I must have that. I love what they have! To what end can we expect to maximize our quality of life? Is your safety and welfare diminished if we all take public transportation to work? Has the jet age really helped society grow? With eight billion people on the earth, we can barely feed ourselves. One does not need to look very far to discover there are societal gaps in all phases of our existence. Wealth gap, hunger gap, housing gap, etc. I'm hoping as a clergyman I can cause people to be sincere in their charity for the less fortunate in our society. The homeless population is increasing, as is panhandling. People don't trust panhandlers because of all the scammers who just don't want to work at a real job. They would rather depend on the kindness of strangers for expendable income. I have it on good authority that some panhandlers can make three to four hundred bucks a day. It isn't enough to give them a handout of money or food. They need help finding a path back to self-reliance. That requires mental and financial assistance. We can't just throw money at a problem. Most homeless people have been completely devalued socially. Society will ask them, why don't you get a job somewhere and improve yourself? At the same time, risk management analysis will not allow the homeless to be hired to park cars or wash dishes. The homeless are being left behind because of bad luck, mental illness, substance abuse, and character victimization.

Enough is enough; I'm going to divinity school. I have got to be able to make a difference at some level, but first, I am going to see exactly how people get into this situation. I found a quiet corner in New York's Central Park, crawled into a thicket, covered myself with a green plastic tarp, and slept on the cold hard ground for two weeks. I foraged for food and water. After the first night, I knew exactly what sights, sounds, paranoia, and fears homeless individuals experience. I could not, however, understand the level of indignity they suffered day after day. People become homeless for a multitude of reasons. PTSD, depression, bipolar, and complications from self-medicating. Many were self-inflicted, but most were a victim of circumstances. A confluence of loss: income, spouse, family member, sanity, personal property, in some combination. There is no possible way to travel exactly the same path as another. The stories are as diverse as the planets of the universe. No two are identical. Like snowflakes from acid rain. Unique but damaged. Yet, victims of homelessness found a way to survive on the bladed edge of society. Soup kitchens, shelters, panhandling, and petty crime/scavenging make up the caustic world of those without substance or sustenance. Nobody cares if the homeless rummage through dumpsters. Rich people throw away the most ridiculous stuff.

One homeless acquaintance, Alice, found a jewelry box full of costume pieces along with a few ten carat diamond rings and one diamond broach. She got $200.00 for the effort. All she got paid for was the gold weight. It's amazing what people throw away. Alice took me to the local coffee shop for breakfast the next morning, where I heard her life story over a few lattes. Alice was a happily married, or so she thought, housewife until her husband suddenly ran off with their twin daughters. Carl, her spouse, unbeknownst to her, took out two mortgages on their brownstone condo and split. The bank took the house via deed in lieu; her BMW was repossessed. With only a high school diploma and no formal residence, no one would hire her to do anything. She had been living in Central Park for three years before I met her. She said the winter nights were brutal. Usually, a shelter would take her in on the below-freezing nights, but many times, all the shelters would be over capacity. Alice had to whore herself out for food or shelter for a warm bed. Clean and sober, she was very attractive. I probably could have laid with her if I tried. Lucky for me, Lena helped me sow many of my wild oats. I did think about Alice more than once. Sadly, I would never taste the fruit of my conjugal fantasy. She froze to death a few days later. Somebody found out about the cash she was carrying and robbed her while she was sleeping.

Apparently, they knocked her unconscious and took everything she had. She died half naked of exposure sometime during the night. I didn't get the news of her death for two days. Another homeless told me.

Barney, another homeless acquaintance, was a truck driver until he lost his job to alcoholism brought on by divorce. His ex-wife, Nora, was screwing around on him with one of his pool league buddies. She took off with his friend, Rick, and they headed to Providence, bought a house and filled it with kids. Nora never even mentioned kids with Barney. She really blindsided him on that one. He thought she was happy. Nora managed a local bakery in the Bronx. He thought things were ok. They had just celebrated their sixth wedding anniversary. Three days later, there was a note on the fridge telling him about the affair and not to pursue her. Barney told me he crawled into a whiskey bottle and stayed there for five years. Their wedding was the happiest day of his life to that point. Nora managed a bakery in the Bronx. Everything seemed ok. Barney thought Nora was satisfied with their middle-class existence. He was gravely mistaken. It took a five-year bender to get over her. He's been clean and sober for two years now. That's progress. He and I were sitting out in the shade of a highway underpass. I listened to Barney laugh and cry over and over again. Nora broke his heart into little pieces. He was so lost without her. She met another man and blew out the door like a quick gust of wind. Just gone, never to return. Not even for any of the divorce proceedings. It was so heartless, the way she left.

Teddy, on the other hand, was angry and would not stay on his medications. When he took his pills on time, he was fine.

But, off his meds was a completely different story. A frequent guest at Bellview Hospital. He got Baker Acted quite a bit. That required a minimum seventy-two-hour stay for observation to determine if the patient was harming themselves or others. I met him on a good day. Teddy was three days released from Bellview. He was a carpenter, fell off a ladder, and broke his back. He had two beers and a sandwich for lunch. They screened his blood at the Hospital. His blood alcohol level was .08. Workman's comp. Denied his claim. It was just a freak accident, even his coworkers backed him up on that. Unfortunately, he did not have the money to fight it out in court. He lost his job, girlfriend, vehicle, apartment, etc. Another statistic has fallen through the cracks of a fractured bureaucratic system. Now, he's homeless and in a lot of pain, both mentally and physically.

I left Central Park and returned to my safe, secure little world, thinking how fortunate I was to have permanent shelter, a means of support, and food security. Our social system in the U. S. is quite delicate at times. There, for the grace of God, I would be homeless and fighting for survival every night. Living day to day, completely dependent upon the kindness and generosity of others.

When I arrived home, I took a long hot shower and then called my local church. I wasn't sure of how much of a warm welcome I would get. I haven't exactly been attending Sunday services regularly for the past twenty-five years.

I pulled up to the church on Monday morning at 8:45. My appt. was at 9. I walked into the church office, and reverend Paulson was waiting for me. I was very surprised. He said he knew that I was coming. I asked, "Did God tell you, reverend?"

"No," he said, "my secretary Katie did." He laughed and said he pulled that joke on everybody. "So, Billy, you are thinking about going to divinity school. Yes, I want to minister to the homeless. That is a very large and noble undertaking, son. Do you believe God has somehow summoned you for this enormous task?" I told him I thought so. I reminded him of that day when the church doors were wide open. I walked in, and we spoke for a while. I told him I didn't think those doors opened by themselves. The Rev. uttered, "That was you sitting in front of the altar?" I nodded. I told him about the eulogy I gave to my friend Keith. He asked if I felt obligated because of my grief over Keith's death. A little, but it's much deeper than that. Then, I went back to the beginning with my biological parents. After two hours of listening to my testimony, all he said was, "That's one heck of a story. You have no idea where your father is?"

"No, I didn't really care for a long time, but now it's time to mend broken fences. He's probably dead. I considered hiring a private detective to locate him for me."

"Billy, one of our members, has a brother who is a private eye. I have his card if you want it."

"Yes, I will take it, thanks."

I figured, what the hell. My ole man's either graveyard dead or muddy drunk in a Tijuana alley begging for his life. The business card read, Robert Lender, private security esquire. I called the number on the card. He wanted a $1000.00 retainer, $500.00 a day plus expenses, with no guarantee I would find him. Two days later, I got a call from Robert. My dad was barely alive, residing in hospice care in New Mexico, of all places, dying from terminal liver cancer. Well, at least he wasn't given a buzzard's funeral. He was allowed to have visitors. So, I hopped a Plane to Albuquerque and rented a car to Las Cruces. He was in Saint Peters Hospice, room 182. I sat in the waiting room for nearly an hour before I actually built up the nerve to go in and see Ronnie. I asked the nurse to show me his room. She said he wasn't doing well at all. Then proceeded to inform me that he was on a morphine drip, there was little time left, and he wouldn't even know I was in the same room with him. I walked into the room, saw his face, and wept. His body was all used up. There was only a shell of the man I once feared so much. I took his hand and could not stop crying. I said, "Dad, you are not going to die alone; I'm here. He died that night in his sleep." The P.A. told me the liver cancer was due to prolonged recreational drug use. Now, he is dead at sixty. Penniless, the only things he came into hospice with were the clothes on his back and a cigar box full of little momentous of his life. As I rambled through the roach clips, one-hitters, and Zippos, I found a safety deposit box key.

I figured I may as well stay around and see to his funeral arrangements. When I went back to the hospice to inquire about any balance due, the nurse said a lawyer had been trying to find me. His office is right here in town. His card read, Dart Smith, Attorney at Law. Really, Dart? I headed over to his office. It was a converted mobile home. The guy was a big-time hunter. Mule deer trophies covered the walls, with the exception of one elk.

Dart told me I had grandparents, and my grandfather, Peter Shaw, was the President and founder of Peterson College in Ft. Worth, Texas. Your grandfather created a family trust; it is an all-expenses paid college education at Peterson College. Well, up to $200,000 over 10 years. All I had to do was enroll in Peterson College and graduate with a four-year degree. They even have a Religion Department. Dart had the contents of Ronnie's safety deposit box emptied for me.

So, I have grandparents. Dart showed me a picture; Grandma was beautiful, with flowing auburn hair and such a warm and inviting smile. Grandpa was a very distinguished gentleman with perfect hair, standing at attention. I would have been a much better man for having known them. Dart reached into his desk removed my father's will, and read the following:

"I, Ronald Alan Shaw, being of sound mind, upon my death, leave all my worldly possessions to my son, William Edward Shaw."

"Wait a minute, I have a middle name, and it's Edward. I like the sound of that. Please continue." Dart kept reading, "This includes my clothes, approximately twenty dollars in cash, and an old cigar box with all my little keepsakes. I have a safety deposit box in one of the local banks in town. In it you will find my copy of an educational trust. It now passes to you. I hope it will somehow benefit you in your life's goals. Good luck to you, son; you are mostly absent but loving nonetheless, father, Ronald Shaw."

I didn't know whether to cry or lash out, so I asked for a drink. Dart obliged me with a double scotch on the rocks. Then, I began to tell Dart how I managed to end up in his office. This was some kind of luck, fate, that brought me here to this point right now.

"Dart," I said, "Did my grandparents even know that I was alive." "No, they had no idea of your existence. Your grandparent's entire estate was sold at auction and donated to Peterson College. The educational trust was a last-ditch effort to get your dad to rehabilitate himself, but that ship sailed the day Ronnie walked out on them."

The next morning, I gathered the contents of Ronnie's safety deposit box. The trust was there, along with a letter addressed to me.

> *Dear son, if you are reading this, then I am dead. I lived a horrible life full of constant violence and chaos. I will spare you the details of my criminal rap sheet, which is extensive. I did go to rodeo prison and broke my arm bull riding. Let's just say I made lots of mistakes up to now. Son, I know you don't owe me anything. But, if you were to graduate from college, my existence would at least have meant something by bringing you into the world. Only now, at the end of my life, do I sorrowfully regret not cherishing our relationship. I just hope that someday you will maybe find it in your heart to forgive me of all the hardship and frustration that I thrust upon you and your mother. Yours could not have been an easy life. I do sincerely hope that you find some degree of happiness.*
>
> *In loving grace, Dad*

Well, what am I supposed to do with that? How do I begin to sequence all the emotional scarring that went on during my adolescence? I cannot remember one instance when Ronnie was a positive influence in my life. He verbally abused me all the time. The very few times that we were alone together, he just sat on the couch in the living room or a lawn chair out in the backyard. Drinking cheap beer and doing bong or pipe hits. I would just climb up a tree or hide under the trailer until he passed out or went out somewhere. We never talked. He yelled, and I would either cry or run away or both. But I learned quickly that crying did nothing but piss him off even more. I just stayed out of sight. It was easier. I think my therapist described our relationship as highly dysfunctional. Well, at least Marie made sure I ate something. Cold cereal in the morning and hot dogs, with mac n cheese at night. It wasn't much, but it kept me from starving. Sometimes, when she wasn't high or turning a trick in the bedroom, we would sit in front of the TV, eat buttered popcorn, and watch a cartoon DVD. It wasn't much, but it was all I had to cling to.

Ronnie hauled ass for good when I was eight. That's when Marie really got into pot and alcohol. Young as I was, I could see the desperation in her face every day as she struggled to keep us fed. Finally, it was too much for her, and she turned me over to the state. The judge was very hard on her for giving up like she did. That was the first day in my life that I just didn't care anymore. I developed an attitude of indifference toward anything and everything I came in contact with. It just didn't matter. Afterall what was the point. I slept in a huge boarding house with thirty-seven other children in the same situation as myself. I just kept my head down and tried not to draw any attention to myself.

That worked for a while until the orphanage bully started giving me a rash of shit every day. Johnny Moss was a big pain in the ass. He was twice my size, and took to beating me up almost every day. Finally, I had enough. I snuck a handful of

35

apples out of the cafeteria and filled up a pair of tube socks, tied the ends together; then I waited until he was alone and venerable. He was outside behind the gymnasium smoking a cigarette, and I laid into him really hard. I never had a problem with him again. I was surprised nobody squealed on me. I guess they had enough of Johnny, too. After that, I never felt sorry for myself or took anyone or anything for granted again. It took several fat lips and sore ribs to learn that lesson, though.

The next year in school, I met Mrs. Wilkes, and my entire life turned around. She tutored me and got my grades up to where I was one of the best students in the entire school. Soon after, I entered foster care. At that moment I really believed all of the chaos in my life was about to come to an end. My foster parents, Betty and Brad, were ok. They were a little strict at first, but after a while, I began to understand where they were coming from. Nothing worth having comes free in life. Ronnie and Marie would have hundreds of dollars one day and be dead broke that same night. The money was too easy to get, so it wasn't real. It had no value for them. All Marie had to do was turn a trick. All Ronnie needed was a mark to hustle or steal from. Brad and Betty were stable. They didn't have tons of money, but that was ok. It was a good life. No chaos. Being rich is great, but not if you don't earn it. Money is a tool, just like a hammer or chisel. Every tool has to be used correctly, or it is ineffective. It also has to be stored properly when not in use, or it creates an unsafe environment to work in, i.e. the money gets spent foolishly.

So, now I was on a fool's errand. Not exactly; I got the money upfront, but to get the prize, I had to graduate. My next action was to seek out the New York law firm of Katz, Finch, and Bassett. Their firm specializes in corporate and family trusts. They were in charge of the trust. Mr. Bassett was very nice for a lawyer. Not the stereotypical uptight New York douchebag. He basically told me I could live as comfortably as I wanted. Basically, $50,000 a year for 4 years. I could even do externships, internships, or school abroad. I told him my SAT scores were nothing to brag about. Not to worry, kid, you are in. Your grampa built the school. It's referred to as a legacy enrollment. I asked if that was fair. That depends on your point of view, now, doesn't it? Apparently so. Nonetheless, I was off to Ft. Worth, Texas. Yee haw!

Chapter 4: Peterson College

I found a modest four-bedroom apartment within walking distance of campus for $500 a month. I ended up with 3 roommates: Paul, Greg, and Veronica. She was dating a varsity linebacker. The guy crushed walnuts with his ear lobes. That was the end of that. I had no chance with her. He was a nice enough guy, just huge.

Tuition and books were free due to my legacy status. It just kept getting better. All I had to pay for was rent, food, and tutors. I needed lots of tutoring in the first year. I did well in high school, but I did not take any college prep courses. I struggled with math and science. English was ok. That was a good thing because I ended up writing a boatload of articles and essays for the Religion Department. Did I mention that any part of the 200 grand leftovers I got to keep as long as I graduated? Yeah, not a bad deal at all.

I decided early on to minor in Theology, which is defined as the study of the nature of God and religious belief. Simple enough, but everyone on the planet has a slightly different opinion about who or what exactly God is. Man, Woman, Deity, or abstraction, I'm still working on that one out for myself. It would be easy to put God in a box and say he or she helps those who help others. So why do horrific things happen to good people? Also, supposedly, everything happens for a reason. Again, theology is only the study of God, not the belief that God exists. God is unseen by the human eye. He or she only exists in our hearts by faith alone. Faith can move mountains. Theologians will tell you where the mountain ends up. Worshipers, no matter the religion or denomination all interpret the word according to their physical histories on earth. They see God according to their surroundings. Otherwise, why would the great one put them in that place and time, and so on? Our relationship with God is cemented into how we choose to live, moral or immoral. Karma, or consequence, may factor into it; more to the point, a series of bad or harmful decisions will ultimately lead to chaos at some point. Burning bridges will eliminate the possibility of turning back. Make damn sure you are on the winning side. My roommate, Paul, was really big on karma. I just couldn't see how killing a cockroach would ever cause me pain and suffering.

While I was at Peterson, I spent much free time volunteering at homeless shelters. It just seemed like a worthwhile thing to do rather than sitting around the apartment playing video games or watching porn. I ran into lots of Alices, Barneys, and Teddys. People who ran out of luck, resources, and faith at the same time. I would show up right around dinner time and just hang out and listen to the stories. Many had just given up trying to reclaim a place in mainstream society. For them, just having a dry place to sleep after a meal, whether on the ground or on a mattress, was good enough. No time clock or regimented lifestyle. The tradeoff was no food security or consistent weather forecast. A bed for the night was what one made of it.

I heard about a guy named Big Red. Apparently, he was completely off the grid. Self-reliant for food, clothing, and shelter. In order to get to his place, you have to cross a ravine on a zip line. Nobody was going to sneak up on this guy. So,

Paul and I decided to pay Red a visit. We brought him a gift. It was an oak-tanned leather shoulder. We were sure he could use it. Getting to his place was a chore. We finally found the ravine and the zip line. That wasn't too bad getting across. The thicket surrounding his cabin was a labyrinth. It was genius how he built the Thing. We weren't exactly sure how we would be accepted, coming unannounced. After he frisked us down for weapons, he introduced himself. Red, as he liked to be called, due to his unmistakable chin whiskers, served afternoon tea promptly at 3 pm. It was the best sassafras tea I ever tasted. He harvested it himself. The biscuits were amazing, too.

Red lived on a two-acre plot in the middle of a huge cattle ranch his grandfather used to work on. Red's father built the cabin and used it as a hunting lodge. Red moved here permeant eighteen years ago. No grid service for power. All his appliances were either wind or solar-powered. It was incredible what he could do with thirty sustained amps of power. The tradeoff was it wasn't always sustained. Sometimes, he would get a cloudy day with no wind. Almost no plastic in sight. The solar panels were his only modern convenience. Indoor plumbing with a full septic system. He was ecstatic over the gift we bought him. He needed the leather for a new pair of winter boots. Red bartered for everything he did not make himself. He thrived through the generosity of his habitat which he was certainly a part of. If the ecosystem were to become unbalanced, he would not be able to cohabitate there. Say, if all the big game were to be poached out. The wildlife would disappear or relocate. Everything is in moderation. Foraging, hunting, agriculture. If Red harvested a tree, he would plant two in its place. All big game kills must be rouges. That way, there would be no chaos within the family unit. The fish and small game have always been abundant in this area. I asked Red if the local authorities were on board with you living in this habitat. They like the help of poachers who like to hunt out of season. It's all private land for miles in any direction. Even small aircraft don't fly around here.

A three-man hunting party came here several years ago and set up an illegal hunting camp. After Red got through with them, they wanted no part of the poaching game anymore. Red said, "Occasionally, visitors like yourselves will show up from time to time. They are usually very respectful of their surroundings. I always serve High tea at 3 pm. You are always welcome if I am around. One must display some measure of decorum. Don't you think?" I agreed. "Will you be staying for the night?" I said, "No, thank you," and we headed back to our cozy consumeristic lifestyle. After returning home, I felt a bit remorseful looking around at all the non-recyclable items that were lying about in the apartment. I told myself that tasteless and dull do not have to be a tradeoff for a simple life interested in consumerism. That was my takeaway from Big Red. Being connected to everyone and everything did not guarantee happiness. There are good and bad aspects hidden in every lifestyle. The trick is to find a way to be happy while diminishing one's carbon footprint. I have a long way to go. It all comes down to wants versus needs. If we put less emphasis on creating a need, our planet would not be in the stink hole mess it is right now. Mother Earth is going to get rid of humans eventually. I'm afraid it may be sooner than later if our species doesn't start to wake up and become more solution oriented. Leather, natural plastic, is plentiful and practical, but petrochemicals are going nowhere in the immediate future. We are too hooked on plastic.

Big Red is an isolated case, few individuals have the survival skills to pull off his lifestyle. They may have some so-called street survival skills, but any survivability in a harsh rural environment without some formalized military training is highly doubtful. It's one thing to camp for a weekend. It's quite another to be completely at the mercy of your immediate rural surroundings. Making a mistake in that environment could prove fatal. Just pissing in one sleeping bag on a night when the temperature is below zero could cause frostbite on the genitals. Very dangerous situation indeed.

Even living on the street means sleeping with one eye open. If not, someone will confiscate everything you have and leave you for dead like Alice. I miss that woman. Once you got past the multiple homeless issues, there was a kind, generous person who could have been a doctor, lawyer, counselor, chef, or anything but a housewife, to a selfish, narcissistic husband. Her ex-husband was ruthless with her. It is as if that was his plan all along. As soon as the girls turned ten years old and could act and think for themselves, Larry took Megan and Marissa away and sued for custody. He claimed Alice was abusive and unfit as a mother. The courts chewed Alice up and spit her out the door. Before Larry left, he put the house and car solely in her name. All she could do was file for bankruptcy and try to start over. On her day in court, she was left standing in front of a judge with a pro-bono lawyer from a legal aide. Larry's attorney made a mockery of Alice's current condition. She was bankrupt, living in a shelter, and she had been Baker Acted twice in Belleview Hospital. The judge saw a completely broken woman on the edge of hope. Larry got full custody of the girls and moved to Florida with his new girlfriend. Alice was completely devastated and barely hanging on by a thread. She probably would have eventually taken her own life if someone hadn't murdered and robbed her that frigid night in January.

I often fantasized, about Alice and I in a non-platonic relationship. I think we would have been good for each other. From our early conversations, I gathered that Larry was a very selfish lover. I'm sure I could have heightened her self-esteem, giving her the warm, embracing intimacy I could see that she longed for. Now, I am left with the memory of her smile and the warmth of her hand in mine. The one kiss I laid upon the corner of her mouth just days before she died will stay etched in my psyche for the rest of my days.

Marriage used to be such a sacred institution. A living testimonial to the love and understanding that two people can share for one another. The vows of fidelity and prosperity that are exchanged signify the bond that both the bride and groom will commit to whatever fortunes may come to pass. How easily vice corrupts the will of even the staunchest character. Broken dreams pass through the marriage bed, separating a confluence of empathy. The bonds are crushed by angst and regret. How can two such loving individuals stray so far from the path set before them. Human nature can give and take with the same ferocity. Alice, my love, we are never to be one united entity on this earth.

College was a good distraction for me. I had to get Alice out of my head. Many nights, I would fantasize about making love to a ghost. Why did that woman have such a powerful hold on me? I think it was the hope that maybe the possibility existed. We could have been much more than friends. I would still pine for her touch. I knew it wasn't healthy to dwell on the past like some teenager full of testosterone-laden puppy lust. I talked to my new therapist about it, and he said I should just go out and get laid. That's not exactly what a religion major wants to hear. So, I prayed about it instead. I had pretty much sold myself on avoiding premarital sex from that point on. The praying did help quite a bit. I started to discover that dwelling on sex and promiscuity was nothing but a distraction to undermine my true short-term goals. Don't get me wrong; I find the female form just as arousing as the next man, but sex without at least the illusion of intimacy is just sport. No real connection, a short, beautiful moment converted to memory, nothing else. For many, that is enough, but not for me. I need to be with a woman who wants a confluence of intimacy. She wants to be lost in my passionate embrace. A woman who can reach the fissures of my beating heart and steady a flame for eternity. I want a loving wife.

Christianity has much to say about marriage and the miracle of procreation. None of us would be here without the miracle that is childbirth. Many days on campus, I have temperate conversations with lovely young women who would love to bed me for a blissful fortnight. Alas, I must slay the lust conceived in their adulterous fantasies. For my constitution must remain pure despite the copious muses that surround my abstinence. Oh yeah, tell that to the guy who invented spandex. He is the bane of my existence and my sticky sheets.

Chapter 5: Alice's Cold Case

I received a snail mail letter of all things from Barney. Apparently, the NYPD has allowed the investigation into Alice's death to go cold as of two weeks ago. There are no new leads, according to the detective in charge of the case. Barney wrote:

I have long suspected a very disgruntled homeless person who went by the street name Swing Low. Apparently, his favorite song. He could be heard singing it from time to time. Alice would turn five-dollar tricks for most of the guys in the park, but not Swing Low. They had a big falling out. I don't know what the beef between them was about. Something about Swing Low was offsetting to Alice. He was tweaking bad on the night she was killed and was wearing her scarf the next day. He told me he found it on the ground. I didn't buy it for a minute. Nobody else had issues with Alice, and we haven't had any newcomers lately. Also, after the night in question, he wasn't tweaking anymore. I wondered where he got the money for booze and smack. It was not the beginning of the month. His checks weren't due for another week. The detective didn't want to hear it. SL is a real piece of work. I'm pretty sure he's dealing drugs. I know for a fact he sells crack. He offered it to me once. You know my vice is alcohol. He's bad news all around. The scarf alone wasn't enough to make new inquiries into her case. The officer just didn't care enough about a homeless victim to pursue the matter any further. I'm sending you this letter because I know that you and Alice were close. If you were wondering, I got your real name and address from the police.

I kind of suspected all along you may not have been homeless. I thought you were a reporter working on a story. The cop told me you were thinking of starting a homeless mission. Forgive me for saying, but you sound like a crusader. That's all fine and good, but just remember that the Crusades didn't turn out all that great for the Nobles in the eleventh and twelfth centuries. Be careful what you wish for.

I like this writing thing. It's very satisfying for me to get my thoughts down on paper. I forgot how much I enjoyed writing in High School. I always got high marks in English. I really enjoyed English Literature. It was challenging and rewarding at the same time. It might have been the only A that I received my entire time in High School. My old man thought hell froze over. Mom was so proud of me. Hey, anything is possible. So, what do I do after High School? I get a job in a gas station/repair shop. It was like an unlicensed apprenticeship. I guess you could call it on-the-job training. Now, almost 15 years later to the day, I am homeless, no vehicle, and living day to day, in and out of shelters. I miss my rig. That sleeper cab was so nice. The long hauls could be grueling.

There was something about being on the road before sunup. Watching the morning sun slowly crest over the horizon gave me a small taste of hope for the coming day. It taunted my senses as the sound of fresh eggs cracked right over the skillet and the smell of bacon frying, and ooh, those delicious flapjacks. Gee, I'm hungry all of a sudden.

It doesn't help me to dwell upon happy things of the past. The once thoughts of blissful conjugal romance. Something I don't foresee ever happening again. Tranquility is now overshadowed by harsh, realistic daily conflicts that I am

forced to overcome just to breach another sunset. To that end,
my friend, I bid you farewell.

I was glad to hear from Barney, even though the circumstances were not the best. He was another very hard luck case who ended up getting exploited by our less than just justice system. I don't think the perpetrator of Alice's death will ever be brought to justice. I don't see the purpose of her demise. It may have something to do with me. Maybe some part of her psyche will benefit another just by me having such deep and loving adoration for her while she was alive and even now. I hope this is to be the case, but for now it is a very difficult situation to try and come to grips with. I still pine for her warm, inviting fellowship. The loss of her will always make me a little pious in remembrance, and I will seek a happy solace with the knowledge that she was my friend.

Before my short little visit to central park those two and a half weeks, I definitely saw justice through white eyes. Justice may be blind, but surely not colorblind. Minority incarceration statistics are appalling. White America will not buy into the fact that the war on drugs is an extension of Jim Crowe. All one has to do is look at the minority gaps in education, wealth, and housing. Alice was defined racially as a person of color. The product of an African American father and an Eastern European mother. They met during World War II, during the occupation of Germany. Her dad was a Tuskegee Airman. A real hero. He died shortly after Alice was born. Her biological father, Samuel Jefferson, struggled to earn a living until a massive stroke killed him while working as a janitor for the New York Department of Education. Her mother remarried a small Italian businessman named Vincent. Now Alice could safely pass as white. Vinnie was the plumber to the wise guys. He kept their plumbing humming and his mouth shut at all times. His customers were extremely gracious to him for that. If anyone in the family had a plumbing issue, they immediately called Vinnie and it was taken care of. The bill always paid straightaway, no questions asked.

So how did Alice end up with Larry, the lawyer? They met in high school. Larry was a three-sport athlete, and Alice was his cute little cheerleader girlfriend. Alice worked full time to support Larry while he went to Cornell. Vinnie was a superb businessman and a loving father to Alice. Larry seemed to be the ideal soulmate for Alice, little did they know. He was no dummy; he got the fifth-highest score on the bar exam. After the girls were born that's when Larry began to drift away from Alice. Many nights, working late or do not come home at all. He did have an hour and a half-commute, but the excuses were getting flimsier and flimsier. You know the rest.

Larry should be arrested for reckless endangerment, wrongful death, or something. It was his complete disregard for her welfare that led to her death. Some people are really good at manipulating the system. Larry was aces in that department. He had no problem padding Alice's credit rating. Then, at just the right moment, leaving her with a grossly upside-down first and second mortgage. It was an absolutely ruthless plan that worked perfectly. Put everything in her name and challenge her competency. Alice told me she never told Larry that her real father was black. I often wondered if he may have found out, and that was why he began to abandon her with such disdain. It kind of makes sense, but how would he have ever found out?

I get pissed off every time I think about it. Then I have to pray away all that anger. Alice did not deserve the life she suffered through. Teddy threatened to kill him once, but I managed to talk him out of it. I told him some people in this world are destined to become the devil's plaything. Just going through life, always landing on their feet no matter how much carnage they inflict upon others. Alice was a forgotten entity passing away into the thinnest of memories by every other being she encountered before I met her. I will not let her existence pass in vain. Somehow, she will be remembered.

At this point, I was into my senior year at Peterson, and I had managed to only use a little over $80,000 of the trust money. I decided to take a semester off and do a little sightseeing in New England. The first stop was the Atlantic shore of Connecticut. A beautiful area with quaint little seaside villages and peaceful tributaries. Further east was Rhode Island. The Ocean State. The apple orchards were more alluring than the beaches, up the Massachusetts cape to Boston. Salem was alive with history. A real ghost town. Then, straight north into Maine. First stop was Kittery. A splendid place. Succulent lobster and incredible chowder. On up the coast to Freeport. Beautiful jagged cliffs are being pounded constantly by massive ocean sea foam. Feeling that spray on my body, chilling me to the bone. I felt so alive. All my senses were brought to the extreme in one specific moment. After a hot shower and more amazing lobster, I headed for the White Mountains. But, no trip to the Northeast U. S. would be complete without a stop at Niagara Falls. Just breathtaking, watching all that water crash down on the base of the Niagara River.

I spent almost eight weeks up there. I met many very interesting people. Diverse as the colors of the rainbow, Italian, Irish, African, Latin, Asian, and Native Americans. New England is a true confluence of American society. No stone unturned. Hustling, bustling to get to and from point A to point B, they never stop.

It was exhilarating and exhausting at the same time. I found what I had lost. A sense of urgency and an intense burning desire to make a difference in the lives of others. I now see my calling to ease the suffering of individuals who have lost the will to be part of something greater than themselves. My mantra is to instill a creative mindset. Creativity is the key to success, happiness, and profound joy. I forgot what it meant to be part of a solution. Barney accused me of being a crusader. So be it. Now, join me in my quest, or step aside.

Creating a startup, especially a non-profit, was a momentous undertaking, even for a college graduate. Almost immediately I reached out for help from the SBA (Small Business Administration). They gave me advice on how to do the things I needed to get started. Even with their help, it was overwhelming. I kept telling myself to find a nice church and live off the tithes and donations. No, then it would be too easy to fall into a soft comfort zone, and I was still way too young for that. I still had some solution-oriented living to do. I managed to find a church willing to hire me as a non-denominational youth pastor. I could draw a menial salary while I put my proposal together to pitch to the local banks. There were seventeen banks and savings institutions in town, and none of them had the slightest interest in bankrolling a halfway house for the homeless. Most of the banks didn't want to deal with all the city's code enforcement issues. The real hurdle was finding an individual sympathetic to the issue of homelessness. There were so many stereotypes attached to the homeless. They all use drugs, steal, and lie about everything. Yes, that is true in many cases. Therapy and rehabilitation will only go so far. In order to truly get someone off the street one must be able to satisfy the individuals long term as well as short term needs.

Most importantly, they have to want to better themselves. All the money in the world won't help someone who doesn't possess any self-discipline. That is the difficult part: getting a person to change their habits to suit a lifestyle that falls within their financial means. That is a very tough sell in this post-consumer. I want it now, society. Living comfortably takes sacrifice and a strong work ethic. Nothing is free in life. It has to be earned.

Chapter 6: The Lottery

The following Monday was to be very important in my young life. Our church leader, Reverend Buchannan, no relation to the former POTUS, was taking a long sabbatical to deal with a family illness. His mother was diagnosed with Multiple Sclerosis, and his father had suddenly passed away from a massive stroke. Being an only child, he brought it upon himself to become his mother's full-time caregiver. Unfortunately, she resides in Omaha, Nebraska. Now, the church elders want me to take over as interim pastor. I graciously agreed. I told the deacons that I sincerely wished that these events could have come at a less solemn occasion. I had not actually delivered a full sermon since college. This would be my first real one to a full congregation. I was quite nervous. I think I did a very smart thing when I called one of my old professors from Peterson.

Dr. Ames was extremely glad to hear my voice. He almost immediately got in his car and made the six-hour trip across Texas to Dickson, LA. We worked on my first sermon for a day and a half. Ray Hicks was an incredible orator and writer. It didn't matter whether it was coming from a classroom or an altar. He was motivating. I must have done well. I was swarmed with hugs and handshakes outside on the church steps. From that moment, I never looked back. I had found a new self-worth. Not so much pride as grace, in the fact that I was now having a substantial positive input in my congregation's spiritual lives. It felt really good to convey a message of hope, peace, and forgiveness. I was now able to Talk the Talk. I'm sure at some future time and place, I will also have to Walk the Walk. Probably sooner than later.

I told myself very early on in college that in order to really instill positive change in others, I would have to wholeheartedly believe in the desire to create value in helping each other. Show all people that together, we create a force more powerful than our sheer numbers alone. An individual can be smart, clever, or resourceful, but if that ingenuity is not used to benefit others, the effort is wasted. Anything I do that doesn't help in some way is a sin. That is my core belief, and I have preached about that many times. It's not about me. It's never been about me, and it should never once, just be about me alone. Now, if only the politicians could buy into that message.

They say miracles happen every day; we just don't look hard enough to recognize them. Babies are born every day. The miracle of life. Flowers bloom and beautify the landscape. Plants and trees grow and pollinate to produce life-giving oxygen. Humans and animals exhale carbon dioxide. One group could not survive without the other. Everything is in balanced moderation.

Ministering to millennials is futile, though, especially on Sunday. Every sermon is an exercise in diversity. I will never stoop so low to judge my followers, but it is certainly complicated. Homosexuals, heterosexuals, people of color, whites, and everyone else have an agenda. Finding a voice for one's individual ideology is paramount. To be heard above the maddening sea of doubt, to shine charismatic knowing your words will live on in later conversation. Lately, I feel that maybe the message is not as fresh on Saturday night as it is on Sunday morning.

My church family is punctual, pious, and evermore enthralled in religious fervor on Sunday. Monday, the catalyst returns, bathed in all forms of self-indulgence. They bow to the internet like a mistress to their master. I get one hour a week to combat the constant bombardment of sin my flock faces. 167 to 1, not good odds.

Constantine must have been at his wits end in 325ce during the Council at Nicaea. All those biblical scholars in one room had to be pure chaos unless there was an open bar. More wine! Phillip is in; Mary Magdalene is out! How they managed to agree upon the final version is beyond me. Truly a divine undertaking.

In all this Christian millennial madness, I was tasked to decide how to spend 463 million dollars!

I should explain. Two months ago, to the day, I was winding up one of my better sermons on tolerance and the power of forgiveness. Following the Sunday service, I met all the attendees at the front door. After that, I gathered all the tithes and offerings that were handed in during the service. Among the envelopes, I noticed one addressed to me personally. I opened the envelope to find a hand written letter inside. As I unfolded the letter, a lottery ticket fell out onto the floor. I picked up the ticket and sat on the first pew to begin reading. I could not believe the words on the page.

Reverend Shaw,

I am writing you this letter anonymously because I happen to be one of the richest individuals in the United States. I have more money than my family, or myself could ever spend in ten lifetimes. As a joke/wager with my son, we both bought a single ticket for last week's Super Colossal Millions Lottery. You may have overheard on the local news that there was one winner and that no person has come forward to claim it yet. You are now in possession of the winning ticket worth approximately 463 million dollars. I have it on good authority that you are a wise, decent, and just person. It is my sincere wish that the prize monies go to help others. Given my financial situation, I feel that you, more than any other, should be the one to disperse the cash payout in a manner you deem fair and equitable.

Thank you,

Anonymous

At first, I thought I was going to be sick. A preacher winning the Lottery. This must be a joke, a very bad joke. I rushed to my car, grabbed my cell phone, and looked up the numbers. It was a match 7 for 7. I thought to myself, "Oh shit." Now, what do I do? I carefully placed the ticket back in the envelope with the letter. It took several tries. My hand was shaking so badly. My heart was racing, pounding through my chest. I hadn't been this nervous since prom night. I mustered up enough nerve to drive home. No seat belt; caution to the wind at this point. I pulled into the driveway, parked, turned the car off, grabbed the letter, and ran into the house. I put the dog out, yanked down all the living room shades, and proceeded to the study, unlocked the bottom drawer of my desk, revealing a bottle of twelve-year old Scotch. I grabbed it and headed for the kitchen table, poured a double, and sat there shaking a little as I sat in the dark, contemplating my next move. The booze was helping to steady my nerves. I lit a candle in the middle of the table. I was shaking so bad I had to light it with two hands.

Why me, God? Really, 463 million. What did I ever do to you? Don't even bring up that blonde in Salt Lake City!

Seriously, how and what am I going to do with all that money? How am I going to cash in the ticket? When the congregation finds out, will they want it all for our church or, worse, for themselves? The last thing this town needs is a bunch of Rolls Royce-driving maniacs carrying Gucci handbags. I was disgusted at the thought. Where should it go? Church missions? Scientific research?

I know one thing. I would love to get my hands on the chicken shit mo)@#$ ^&*()!@ that sent me this ticket. Boy, talk about passing the buck. 463 million of them, to be exact. Well, I have a year to decide. The ticket doesn't expire until then. No, I will have to come forward much sooner than that. Should I lie and say I bought the ticket or that I found the ticket? My salary comes from tithes and offerings. That won't work. It could be deemed misappropriation of church funds, maybe not legally, but morally, yes. I think I better talk to a lawyer.

I desperately wanted to know who sent me this money. There can't be that many people in America worth over 463 million dollars. I googled it, and there are over 3000 billionaires in the U.S., 400 in California alone. He or she might not be a billionaire at all. It could just be someone who only has 10 million or less. Who knows? One fact remains: right now, it's just they and I who know of my situation.

It started to become clear to me that the right thing to do would be to keep a small amount for the church funds. Use a third for foreign missions and the rest for medical research. But, there is always a but. What about the tax ramifications? The ticket was given to me personally. Is it income, or is it a donation? I don't know. Can the ticket be transferred from one person to another? I bet not. The prize money could end up part of a civil suit. A cash payout would be somewhere around 200 million after taxes, maybe. 2 million for the church, 65 million for foreign missions, and 133 million for medical research, or something to that effect.

I also came to the realization that the right thing to do may not be the ethical thing to do. I would have to decide beforehand how many and which research facilities would be receiving a donation. That would take some time. I would not be able to do this alone. Once word got out, our quiet little town would start to take on a carnivallike atmosphere. Who would benefit from this possible media circus? I don't think anyone would. I believe the solution lies in finding a way to distribute the money in such a way that won't cause undue stress for all the parties involved. Basically, what would Jesus do? I think Jesus would return to Caesar what belongs to Caesar. I dipped a corner of the lottery ticket into the candle flame and watched it glow red, yellow, orange, blue, purple, and eventually black. Problem solved.

I vowed to God that I would take today's events to the grave. I prayed I did the right thing. It didn't really matter now;

that ticket was a pile of gray ashes lying in the bottom of a candlestand. I had another drink and fell asleep on the couch. I woke up just in time for evening services. Tonight's sermon was on the power of conscience. How appropriate. It never ceases to amaze me how a Sunday sermon always seems to be just what the congregation needs to hear right at that particular moment in time. On that day, I needed it, too. My sermon went as follows:

Good evening, folks. God bless you all for coming. Tonight, I would like to discuss the power of conscience. We all have one buried in ourselves. Most of us keep it locked away someplace safe. Some keep it closer to the heart than others. I have heard conscience described as a human moral compass. I'm sure most of us would agree with that analogy. It's fair to say most of us base the decisions we make and the actions we take around the premise of good versus evil. Everyone has some level of gray area they struggle with. I believe that the gray area is in a constant battle with conscience. The gray separates goodness from sin. We've all heard the debate: if it's fun, if it tastes good, or if it feels good, then it has to be sinful. We, as Christians, can enjoy the benefits of life. Just nothing too extreme. Anything taken in an unhealthy overabundance is perverse. Having one light beer at a neighbor's BBQ is not a sin. Now, if you don't like the taste of beer and you are only doing it to impress someone else. That would be bowing to peer pressure. What if you don't know whether you like beer or not? Drinking your first beer at a friend's house because your curious how it tastes, would that constitute a sin? That would most assuredly not be defined as a sinful act. Becoming visibly inebriated would be. Everything is in moderation.

But alcohol is a mind-altering substance; I have heard it called the big sneak; one or two drinks the first time is not considered alcoholic behavior. Consistent consumption of alcohol, say 5 to 8 drinks a week, could lead to alcoholism. Bottom line, booze impairs judgement. Now you are back in the gray, dancing around perverse behavior. Even the medical community doesn't recommend frequent consumption of alcohol.

Obesity is another sneak. Putting on 5 pounds a year doesn't seem like much, but over 20 years, that's 100 pounds. Everything is in moderation. Sex, money, yes, money can be an enormous vice. It must always be used wisely and in moderation, given consideration of the circumstances.

Time, or more to the point, free time, like money, should not be spent foolishly. Don't veg out in front of the TV when there are chores left to do. A creative mind engaged in a constructive task should produce a worthwhile result, and if it's something you are passionate about, it cold be fun. Me, I like doing leather work. I do sometimes sell the projects I make, or give them away as gifts.

In conclusion, conscience is what guides us in every moral decision we make. Don't decide hastily. Give yourself a chance to consider the consequences of your decision. The choices we make in life will affect our lives and greatly impact the lives of others we come in contact with, both directly and indirectly. Look, if you are truly at your wits end achieving a decision about something. Ask yourself, what would Jesus do?

Thank you, Jesus. I just pissed away 463 million dollars. What the hell did I do that for? I am going to be kicking myself in the ass over that one for a long time. I have got to be the biggest moron in the world but for my conscience. Yes, my all-knowing overtly guilt-laden moral compass. The money, even though the beckoning of my hands, would have eventually done more harm than good. I hope it was God's will that guided me to destroy the winning ticket. I followed my conscience. I hope that was enough.

I now knew what next Sunday's sermon would be about. God's purpose for us while we exist on the earth. Now, all I had to do was write it. Tricky things, these sermons. The message must be strong and clear without being crass or condescending. People aren't stupid, at least most of the time. They can smell crap when it comes into their general vicinity. It has to strike home, especially if the message doesn't necessarily resonate with their lifestyle or character. That is where the morality comes in. If scripture is telling us something is immoral then it has to be, but it is how the individual interprets that message which can lead to temptation or salvation. Hence, our conscience is now front and center. The message is clear. Now, how far into the gray are you willing to step? As for myself, I'm usually not covered in gray until the following Saturday morning. Some are drenched in gray by Monday morning immediately following a Sunday sermon. Human nature, in all its complexity, is as random as the stars. God wants all his children to be content, pious, and obedient. None of which relates to residing in the United States of America in the twenty-first century. As artificial intelligence becomes more prevalent in our daily lives, the temptation to become more sedentary increases. Gaps in work ethic are already noticeable between baby boomers and millennials. College students today don't have the tenacious grit of their ancestry. This is not an issue as long as the technology holds up. Right now, our power grid is fragile. Venerable to climate change, geopolitical insurgency, terrorism, etc. God tells us to get our house in order. We need to comply sooner than later.

My transition to interim pastor has been an eye-opening experience. Most days, I feel quite overwhelmed. So many questions unanswered. Delegating a task to a church volunteer can be very futile at times, with only three full-time employees and one part-time worker. It is extremely difficult to keep from missing the mark. We did manage to get a volunteer to take over as youth pastor. One of the Deacons has graciously filled that position. That leaves me as the man at the center of all things spiritual. I must get better organized. I will have to put the homeless ministry on a back burner for now. I don't want to do that, but unfortunately, I don't have a choice. People are counting on me for leadership.

My thoughts still dwell on Alice. Why does this woman have such a profound hold on my heart? She has been gone for almost a year now. I fall asleep clutching to the short, robust gatherings we had. The walks in Central Park and the long lunches, during which we shared some of our innermost thoughts and passions. Her favorite ice cream was a rocky road; her favorite color was pastel pink, and I can still smell her perfume, Roses Blush. She adored Shrimp Scampi. The kiss I gave her on the corner of her lips caused a rage of carnal thoughts to race through my body. It was the most erotic semi-platonic kiss I have ever made. I wanted to make love to Alice over and over again. Our naked bodies tangled over one another, kissing, touching, verbalizing the engorged ecstasies passing between our severely titillated bodies. I wanted to be with this woman all my days on the earth.

Why, God, why is she gone? I know she probably never regained consciousness after receiving a blow to the head, but still, why did she have to die? The thief probably could have stolen her money without bashing her on the head. Was it a disgruntled John, perhaps a jealous girlfriend of one of her Johns? No, I know who killed her, and Barney can lead me to him. Swing Low is my bane. My callous, my infectious boil. The itch I can't scratch. Vengeance is mine, Romans 12, I will do the Lord's bidding. The man must be put under. I could kill the man very easily. From my vantage, it would be a justified homicide. The police have allowed her death to go unpunished. That is not justice that a man should take a life for $180.00 in cash. Money which was surely spent foolishly on vices. Of which he had many. I will avenge her. He will take a long time to die.

I assume Barney is still residing in central park. All that was listed on the return address was B. Holmes, Central Park, NYC. I would have to travel there in person. I could take the redeye from New Orleans. Dispose of Swing Low and return in less than twenty-four hours if I choose to do so. As of now, I am still in the gray.

Several months later, I received another letter from Barney updating me on the Swing Low situation. He wrote that SL was really drunk about two weeks ago and spouting off about how he alone was going to clean up central park one crack whore at a time. He said he started over a year ago taking care of this menace his way. Billy, my friend, that was enough to convince me, but I recently lost three fingers on my right hand to frostbite, and I am not good in a fight anymore. I will need a wingman to get the job done.

I could justify killing during time of war, but Barney is asking me to take part in the slaying of an unarmed man for revenge. That is a little out of my league. It's true; if he is going around killing homeless women in Central Park on suspicion of being a crack whore, something must be done if the police are not putting any real effort into the case. Human lives are being eliminated because of circumstance and misfortune. That's not vigilantism, it's serialism. This cannot be allowed to continue. I must investigate the situation myself.

Barney wrote six women have gone missing without a trace. The ages range from sixteen to twenty-eight. For some reason, the women thirty and over have not been targeted. The NYPD has written it off, saying the women have moved on to greener pastures. All of these girls were the same as Alice, forced into prostitution to survive. Billy, I know somebody has had to see something. Two of these girls I knew personally, and they weren't planning to go anywhere. In fact, one had a steady John who was paying her really well. I don't have anything on Swing Low the D.A. would be interested in, but man, every time I see the guy, he scurries off like his ass is on fire. He's dirty, I know it. I managed to get myself a cellphone I am just waiting for the first of the month so I can buy some time to put on it. You can expect a call from me around the 3rd or 4th of next month. Talk to you soon.

This was really starting to get complicated. Why hasn't the NYPD done anything about all these missing girls? Where are they running to, or are they being kidnapped? Could this be a sex trafficking scam? These girls may be collected and sent elsewhere to be exploited as sex workers. Swing Low may be the Central Park connection. How is it that nobody is observing this? Maybe they are just too afraid to come forward. I will bet many of these women are illegals. That would make it the perfect crime. Confiscate people who aren't supposed to be here anyway. It's a win for the police and the pimps. Swing Low knows what happened to Alice; he has to. I should hear from Barney in a couple of days. So, for my part I will have to come up with some legitimate reason for going back to NYC. That won't be easy. I could tell my congregation the truth and say I need to take a sabbatical to go and destroy a serialist in NYC. Half of them would faint, and the other half would help me pack. Honestly, I am not ready to commit to that kind of retaliation.

I find it appalling what happened to Alice and those other women. On the surface, Alice's death definitely doesn't fit the profile of the other disappearances. I would like to know what the rift between Swing Low and Alice was, though. It had to have something to do with sex, money, or both. Swing Low doesn't seem to be the type of man who took rejection very well. Hopefully I will know more when I talk to Barney. He seems to be connected to many homeless issues in and around Central Park. Like how are homeless people able to hide out there and stay undetected? It's not a very big area. Why aren't the park police more involved in controlling the vagrant population in the park? Like all hiccups in life, this, too, shall pass at some point.

Chapter 7: Candy, My Muse

The big mirror in my bathroom keeps telling me it is time to get a haircut. That means a trip to my hairstylist, unlicensed therapist, Candy. Smart woman that Candy, I get in her chair and talk, probably more than I should. It doesn't matter the topic. She just absorbs every word she hears. That is a gift very few people possess. Candy can take the words that are spoken to her. Not that she is the truest form of wisdom in my life, but the woman is easy to talk to. She understands the value of active listening. I tell her everything. Most times I have to change the names or speak in hypotheticals for obvious reasons. I have found it difficult to deal with work-related issues since Rev. Buchannan, Arthur, left to take care of his mother, who, from the last update, needs Arthur just to get through the day.

Candy is a sage and a friend at the same time. My congregation comes to me with everything from what outfit to wear at a summer BBQ to surviving the death of a relative. It's usually the fashion questions that I struggle with, and Candy just laughed at my listless fashion sense and said, "You, dork, tell them to wear something fun and comfortable. If there's a pool at the house, don't forget the bathing suit." I wonder how many people sit in this very chair that I'm occupying right now, and I absolutely cherish the comradery and platonic intimacy that transpires during a simple cut, wash and set. Everyone enjoys having someone pay extremely close attention to them once and a while. Truly, at the end of the day, it's not about me. That doesn't mean that I can't be the recipient of some grand form of loving-kindness. Kindness, respect, and empathy have gotten lost in our ridiculous, reactionary, double-espresso lives.

Kids fascinate me sometimes. Their problems don't have the same depth as our own, but to them, they are extremely heavy and demanding. I started to tell Candy about a seventeen-year-old girl in my senior youth class. I will refer to her as Mary. Mary is struggling with whether or not to have sex with her first real boyfriend; well, call him Joseph.

This one is cut and dry as far as the church is concerned. No premarital sex. That's a difficult message to sell when a mountainous sea of endless hormones tells young people to go for it. I told Mary that her body was obviously ready for sex, but her brain was not. Sex without a sustained long-term commitment, i.e., marriage, is like a birthday cake without a meal beforehand. It's sweet and satisfying for the moment but not fulfilling. In order for a relationship to be worth a damn, it has to be built on trust and respect. Loving someone with all your heart and soul is important, but it is never enough. I asked Mary, "This man, Joseph, that you are infatuated with. Does he feel the same way about you?"

She nodded.

"How do you know for sure? Has he talked about marriage?"

Mary said, "He says he loves me and wants to make love to me to prove it."

I informed her that he had no intention of following through on any shallow promises he may have mentioned in the heat of the moment. The fact that Joseph is seventeen also convinced me that she needed to have a long, serious talk with that boy and find out what his intentions really were. Meeting the parents is never a bad idea at that age. That will say a lot about his character as a young man. They are both seniors in high school. I told her they needed to talk about short, and long-term plans, college, military, or trade school. That was the Elephant in the room. Joseph has aspirations of being a software engineer, writing video games. She talked about becoming a medical technician. Something in the medical field. I told her that what she's going through is completely normal no one knows what the next day will bring. I get up some mornings, and I'm petrified about things until I turn on the coffee pot, and then I sit down and pray to God for the wisdom to help others. I reminded her that it's not really about us. There is an inner peace that we all can achieve when we do something good for someone other than ourselves. Even just holding the door for someone walking into a building. Human kindness is electricity for the soul. It is also healthy. We humans are constantly creating things. Some good, some bad, but we never stop. Mary, the key is to always be solution-oriented. When faced with a problem, don't ignore it; that issue is not going to go away. Now, you can pray for the answer. That always helps, but remember, the answer may not appear in the context that you expect. It's not always obvious when God speaks to us. Most of my problems are solved when I share the load with him. Mary, I'll let you in on a little secret. There isn't a human problem or dilemma on this earth that the answer is not written in the bible. All things are achieved through prayer.

Mary left my office a little confused; what did she expect? I'm not a sex therapist. I just hope she doesn't come back to me in then months with an infant in her hands, unless she is babysitting. Children push boundaries, attempt stupid stuff, and experiment with sex and controlled substances.

I told you Candy was a good listener. She agreed with most of what I was saying, but I should have asked about planned parenthood. "Those people are extremely good at counseling young women through those kinds of ordeals." Candy elaborated, "My first time was right after my eighteenth birthday. I was lucky; it was his first time, too. We were both done pretty quickly. He was fascinated with my body. I liked his body as well. We were strictly in missionary positions. I was really surprised I had an orgasm. My mom told me it doesn't always happen the first time. I brought my vibrator with me as a backup, along with a few condoms. He really liked it when I put it on him. Billy, we are never going to be on the same page when it comes to unmarried sex. I see nothing wrong with it. I like the cake without dinner analogy, but I have managed to share a very high level of intimacy with several men and one woman, but not at the same time."

"Woman!" I said, "Candy, did you say woman?"

"Yes. Woman. Now relax before you get your tighty-whities in a twist. She was a co-worker at another salon. We only dated for about two months."

I was taken aback, "Candy, how could you be attracted to a woman?"

"Look, dude," she said, "probably for the same reason you are. The female form is very alluring. We were both very effeminate women. Sex with her was amazing. She knew exactly how, when, and where to touch me to maximize my climax. It was purely sexual. She was not a cuddler at all. She taught me how to vocalize my sexual experience. I have only been with one man who even came close to that level of intimacy. But as you so eloquently point out, it's not enough to sustain a real relationship. Morgan was a truly gifted lover. She was very incomplete, though. She was very shallow as a friend and not a very good listener. Finally, I had had enough. So, my great experiment on the other side of the fence failed. The grass was definitely greener but very bitter at times. You know, you're the first man I ever talked about Morgan with. Ok, Mr. homophobe, when was your first experience."

I retorted, "Well, I never slept with a man if that's what you are asking. My first time was with a woman named Lena. I was a senior in high school. She was twenty-two, beautiful, and also not a cuddler. The things that she taught me, I will never forget. I learned how to make love, how to share in physical pleasure, and how to respect the time we had together. Lena knew how to get me extremely excited and keep me there until she was ready. Then, it was like riding a tidal wave raging through our simultaneous climaxes. Oh boy, I'm going to be doing some extra praying tonight for this conversation. For me, it ended bittersweet. She went back to grad school and got her PhD in British Literature. I lost touch after she graduated."

Then she asked me point blank, "Billy, have you ever thought about getting married?"

I replied, "Well, right now is not a very good time for me. I have a lot going on right now, and you are the only wife material I have come across in quite a while." Candy sighed, "Oh, Bill." She immediately gave me a very passionate kiss and stroked my crotch in an extremely arousing manner. I kissed her back. I had to. She stoked fiery passions in me that I had long forgotten. When she broke off the kiss and came up for air, I told her this was so wrong, but it was too late. I lost one head and gave in to the other one. We scampered off into her bedroom and lay with each other for several hours. It felt really good. No, fantastic. I left her salon with two-thirds of a haircut and a smile on my face that a jackhammer couldn't pry off. Well, I did it. Now, I am the adulterous hypocritical small-town preacher. I know Candy is not the marrying type; she told me several times. What's worse I have to go back and let her finish my haircut. I will have to go back before Sunday for sure.

What is it about sex prior to marriage that God is so upset about? No, I know, it's the commitment thing. If we are not willing to commit our lives to each other, then we will just end up hurting ourselves, our families, and our friends. If one is not going to cook the meal, eat the meal, and do the dishes after, then they don't deserve the delicious dessert. Sex should enhance the intimacy in a marriage, not be the foundation for one.

That said, I am so stuck on her right now. Maybe I can convince her to commit to me. Not for nothing, I did rock her world for several hours. I have to talk to her. I have to know her thoughts about me.

I headed back to her shop Saturday afternoon. I ended up waiting until she finished two people ahead of me. A wash and set, then a wet cut. I got back in the chair. And she was all over me again. I stopped her this time and asked her what her intentions were. She said, "What, am I talking to your father? It should be obvious I want to screw your brains out."

"Candy," I said, "I want to as well, but you know how this is going to end if we don't make a commitment to each other."

She snapped back, "Billy, you are treating me like I am the horny boyfriend who wants a free supply of milk without buying the cow. Billy, I like you. The day before yesterday was incredible. No man ever made love to me like that before. I want you right now, tomorrow, and the next. Let's just see where it goes for a while." I agreed, "Ok, but can you at least finish my haircut first."

She said, "Sure, honey." Then she kissed me again; this woman had a severe hold on me.

Candy is not what you would call a good, wholesome Christian woman. The lesbian incident aside, she is nowhere near the stereotypical preacher's wife. She has almost no experience with scripture. I guess that can be learned. The question is, will she be willing to learn? I went back to her place after dinner, and of course, we ended up in bed together, and it was probably the best sex I ever had. I have got to get this woman to marry me.

I asked her, "Candy, how much do you know about the Bible?" She scoffed, "Which book? James? A realist. Tells it like it is. Ok, what about Daniel?"

She sighed, "Daniel. He's perplexing. A very devout no-nonsense profit who also didn't pull any punches. There is a reason he was an advisor to so many kings. He was a very

71

intelligent man. We could use someone like him today advising some of these foolishly absurd politicians running things now."

I asked, "Candy, how do you know so much about the Bible." She continued, "My uncle Matt was a preacher in Shreveport. He passed away about six years ago. I grew up there, and we went to his church every Sunday, rain or shine. Some of the Sunday School lessons stayed with me. Personally, I like James and Luke. They are definitely my favorites; why do you want to know? As if I couldn't guess? You aren't in love with me already, are you? Look, sweet gentleman, it takes a lot more than two good lays and some stimulating conversation to get me across the aisle. You've got your work cut out for you, but you are definitely on the right track. I feel incredible when we are together, and I don't want that to go away. So, let's take it slow for now. We can get together once or twice a week and see what happens. I think it would be ok for us to be seen having lunch together. We will have to sneak around for everything else for a while. Don't you agree?"

Puzzled, I said, "Candy, how did you?"

She said, "You are a guy, everyone the same, dick like a hood ornament; wherever it goes, the car follows. I know exactly how to stimulate that luscious cock of yours. Gimmie a month, and you will never want to leave my bedroom again. Billy, I care about you very much at this point. You are a good, loving, passionate, unselfish man, the first one I have come across in a very long time. I want this thing to work out between us just as much as you do. I think I can be very happy with you. The question is, will your church accept me as a preacher's wife and a career cosmetologist? I'm not sure. Luckily, most of the women in your congregation come to me to get their hair done. That certainly can't hurt our cause. Lucky for us, I have only been in this town a few years. I haven't been labeled as some kind of gold-digging mistress. What do you think?"

I said, "Well, Candy, I think you pretty much covered it." She barked, "Ok, lover man, get in that bedroom and take your clothes off." I nodded, and off I went.

Members of my dutiful congregation have observed Candy and me having lunch around town. So far, there have been no threats to disembowel themselves in the middle of Main Street unless I stop seeing Candy. The real test will come on Sunday at church when she arrives. I don't have to worry about her biblical knowledge. She may have read the bible cover to cover more than I have.

The Bible has always fascinated the heck out of me. There are sixty-six canons written by almost as many authors. A few of the books still remain anonymous. I often wondered if that was on purpose. Hebrews, for instance, no one actually knows who wrote it, yet it remains very well-read and topical. The Bible is a vast preponderance of wisdom. Open it to any page, and somewhere in that unfold is a relevant passage. It really works.

Let's just say for fun, Candy and I got married. Would she want kids? I don't want kids. They are messy, sticky, and ask about a million questions. They never shut up. They always want something, usually when you are dead tired. Also, they only want unconditional love, to constantly please you, and their smile makes you melt with joy. That's all they ever do. Who would ever want to deal with that constantly? Oh, I don't know, maybe just about anybody. Forget the fact that this geopolitical nightmare is not the ideal. Children are an oasis among the dunes. Candy can't have children; her fallopian tubes are inoperative. I suggested adoption, and she pointed out the obvious. She had her clients, I had my congregation, let's leave it at that. She made a good point. Focus on the matters at hand. Little did she know I planned to pop the question at our next ice cream social. One of the deacons tossed me a throw pillow. I dropped it down on the floor and shoved a big rock in her face, and she said yes. Everyone cheered and congratulated us. It was a small ceremony; she had no family to speak of, nor did I, so naturally, it ended up being the biggest wedding in town. The sanctuary was at capacity. We cleared almost $8,000.00 in wedding gifts. It helped being connected to almost everyone in town. The reception didn't cost us a dime, we held that in the fellowship hall. Candy looked stunning in that dress. OMG. I thought I was going to bust something when she came down the aisle. That was the day Candice Wilhelmina Doyle married William Edward Shaw.

I thought it was never going to happen. After my volatile childhood, I figured marriage was completely out of the question. We honeymooned in Daytona Beach. Two weeks of beaches, nightclubs, charter fishing, and nookie, nookie, nookie. After arriving home, we slept for a day and a half. It was an amazing honeymoon, but we were both dog-tired and glad to be home.

Chapter 8: Barney's Update

The next morning, I went to the church office for my first day back. On my desk was another letter from Barney.

He wrote:

Billy, the total of missing women is up to 18 as of last week. Swing Low has been missing for a while, too, but he could be hiding out in the old subway tunnels. I heard some people tell me there is a whole other city down there. I have never seen it myself. I have a cell phone now. My number is listed below. Please give me a call. Only during the day, it's too dangerous to call me at night. Somebody might hear it ring or me talking on it. these things are like gold around here. I have to be really careful when and where I use it. Someone is systematically kidnapping young women from the park. I don't think SL is the leader of the mob that's doing it, but he fits into it somehow. Call me during the day around 10:00 am Eastern time. Thanks, Barney

517-844-2188. Remember, after 10 a.m

I called the number, and Barney answered. I said, "Barney, it's Billy. Can you talk?" He said no, "I will call you later." Click. I texted him, inquiring as to his safety at this point. He sent, OK. I waited for his call. I read the letter again, and the thing that stuck in my mind was how Swing Low fit into all this. I think he is just a front, finding the victims for someone else. But who? There has to be a witness to one of the abductions. Candy is not going to like it, but I am going to have to go to NYC and investigate further. Barney is getting up there in years, and he recently lost three fingers on his right hand. That can be easy to deal with, especially at night. The cold weather, I am sure is aggravating as heck sometimes.

I headed over to Candy's shop, and when I arrived, I had a seat in the waiting area. When her client left, I said, "Mrs. Shaw, are you free?"

"Sure, Mr. Shaw. Do you want to lie down in the back for an hour or so?"

"No, sweetie, I need to talk to you about something that has come up."

"Honey, what's going on."

"Remember I told you how I spent some time in Central Park, posing as a homeless person? Barney sent me another letter. The total missing is now eighteen. I need to go there and find out what is truly going on."

"Billy, you are not still hung up on Alice, are you?"

"No, it's nothing like that. I just want to find out what happened to her and all the other girls who keep disappearing. There is definitely something sinister taking place there, and the NYPD could care less. Even the Park Police are ignoring the situation. I want to reconnect with the detective who was originally assigned to Alice's case."

"Can you call him?"

"Well, yes, I could, but that doesn't really convey the message I am trying to send. I want the police to realize the gravity of the situation. I will probably have to threaten to go to the press to get anything done. I could write an editorial and send it to my journalist friend. Geraldine is her name. She is one of my college roommates and sister. She graduated from NYU in the top five in her class. She has been there for quite some time. She writes a couple of columns a week. Like I said, I could try and use that as leverage to get the NYPD off their butts."

Candy inferred, "Ok, how long will we be gone."

I quipped, "We? No way. I can't let you go with me; it's too dangerous."

"Oh, I see! Too dangerous for a woman, not for a man. Is that it?"

"Candy, please, these are dangerous people I may come into contact with, and they appear to be specifically targeting attractive women. They could use you to get to me."

"Billy, you know I grew up on a farm. I am an excellent marksman. I will admit I'm not quite the shootist that you are, but I am certainly no slouch, even under fire. You may need some help on this one. Let me help you."

"You're not going to let this go, are you? What about your clients?"

"What about your congregation, huh?"

I told Candy I didn't plan to be gone that long and that I would do everything in my power to avoid any violent altercations. I just want to go to New York and find out what exactly is going on. These people will be a whole lot more willing to talk to Barney and me than the cops. I have to go there and talk to Swing Low. He is definitely hiding something. I suspect he is up to his neck in whatever's going on.

"Billy, did you just call me attractive a minute ago?"

"Yeah, I did. Attractive, sexy, beautiful, voluptuous, ravishing, splendid, beautiful."

"You said beautiful twice." Candy moved closer to me and wrapped her arms around my neck and shoulders. Then she slid her hands around and let her fingers follow the contours of my jawline. I told her It definitely bared repeating in your case. "Kiss me, you sweet hunk of man, you." We embraced for several hours, then packed up for NYC.

We flew out of New Orleans on Sunday evening, hoping to return sometime on the following Saturday. We wanted to give the impression it was just a mini vacation to the Big Apple. The first order of business would be to contact Barney and then head over to Central Park. I called him on his cell, and we agreed to meet at a coffee shop one block from the park's main entrance at 3 pm. Candy and I arrived at 2:30 and ordered food and drinks while we waited for Barney. 3:30 pm, and still no Barney. Finally, he showed up at twenty to four.

"Sorry, Billy, I got hung up, and my battery phone needs a charge."

We sat and listened as Barney gave us the entire 411. He went on to say these women just before dawn and never a trace of anything they owned. Bags, shopping carts, tarps, and even food scraps. It's like they were never here. Someone doesn't want to leave a single clue that they were there. I asked how they could be kidnapping people. Wait, they're not being kidnapped; they are being lured away, conned into leaving.

One question is, what are they being baited with? It's got to be food and shelter. Barney said it had to be food and shelter.

I would pack up all my shit and follow someone for that. Me too.

Second question: where are they going?

"For that, my friend, I haven't a clue. None of the local shelters know either." Honestly, Barney said, "The shelters aren't much help because people revolve in and out of those places too fast."

"What about race? Is that a factor? Are they targeting one race over another?"

"No, Asian, African, North, South American, Caribbean, it doesn't matter, just that they are young and homeless."

"Barney, do you think Alice was killed because she knew something?"

"It's possible. I think Swing Low might have disappeared because he knew too much, and the people he worked for didn't trust him to keep his mouth shut. He would start talking after about half a bottle of liquor. I'm sure it got him killed."

"Let's go talk to that Detective; Breen was his name, right?"

"Yeah, that's him. A bloody lot of good it will do."

"Come on, Barney, humor me this once."

"Ok."

So, we headed down to the nineteenth precinct, filtered our way through the door, and waited our turn with the desk Sgt. I asked if we could speak with Detective Breen. The Sgt. asked us what it was in reference to. I said the Alice Reynolds case. About ten minutes later, a uniformed officer came down and immediately started asking us who we were and why we were so inquiring about the case. I showed him my credentials and told him we were curious if there had been any new leads in the investigation. He said no in a very abrupt manner. I asked if Det. Breen was available and again, he said no. "Thank you, Officer Pitts, for your time. Do you have a card that I could have?" He reluctantly gave me his card. We left.

"Barney, do you know what Det. Breen looks like?"

"Oh, yeah."

Ok, the man has to eat sometime. We will have to smoke him out. Breen, he's Irish, probably, yes. Well, that means we need to find a cop bar that serves good Irish whiskey. Candy said, "Allow me."

The next handsome uniformed officer who walked out of the precinct deliberately ran into him and fell to the ground.

"I'm so sorry, miss. Are you ok?"

"I think so, but I could really use a belt of Irish whiskey right now."

"My name is Chris McGill, and I know just the place, about 2 blocks up the street from here if you would care to join me."

"Are you sure you are ok? You aren't cut or bleeding, I hope."

"No, not a scratch, just a little shaken up. Nothing a shot or two wouldn't cure."

"Barney, follow the lady."

We were no sooner in the door, and who did we spy at the bar hoisting a boilermaker? None other than Det. Breen. I pulled up next to him and politely asked what that drink was that he so eloquently poured down; he looked at me and asked if I had ever drunk a boilermaker before. I lied and said I had not.

"Well, barkeep, set us up." I slammed mine in good Irish fashion. After that I told him that I came here with an agenda. My name is Reverend William Shaw, and my wife, associate, and I are in the city to follow up on the Alice Reynolds case.

"Ok, first, I never met a man of the cloth who could pound a boilermaker like that."

"I told him every preacher was something before they took to the cloth."

"True."

"So, Detective, what about Alice?"

"Nothing, I'm afraid. We had a suspect, but he was in Belleview Hospital that night."

"Was it Swing Low."

"Yes, how did you know about Swing Low?"

"Barney here suspected him for quite a while, but you say he was definitely in Belleview the night of her death. He was there until 9:30 the next morning. Then it couldn't have been him."

"No."

"Swing Low is back in Belleview again; he ends up there every time he runs out of medication. He served in Afghanistan, and it did a number on him. Lots of PTSD issues. He's not talking to anybody."

"Do you think he might talk to another veteran?"

"Anything is possible. It might help us if you could get him to come in and give us a statement."

"What about all the young women who keep disappearing from the park?"

"That is an ongoing investigation. *The Vice* squad is looking into it, but just like Alice, there's nothing to go on. The disappearances are just random enough to look like they are just wandering off."

"Look, Frank, can I call you Frank?"

"Please call me Billy. There has to be a connection. Barney says people occupy the old subway tunnels under the streets. Is there any truth to that?"

"A lot of rumors, but that's all it is, just talk. Plus, a few ghost stories. Until someone comes forward who has actually seen an abduction, our hands are tied. Billy, I have to warn you not to interfere in an open investigation without proper authority. That's pretty serious stuff."

"I know, Frank, the last thing we want is to put anyone, including ourselves, in Jeopardy."

"By the way, how did you find me?"

"See that pretty Redhead at the end of the bar. Hi honey, have you been waiting long."

"No, are you finished talking to Detective Breen?"

"Oh yes, we can go. Thank you, Officer McGill."

So, we were right back to square one. I don't know how much it will help, but we at least have to talk to Swing. He definitely knows something. Whether he will talk about it is the key. Visiting hours are 8 am to 8 pm. What do we have to lose? I could not believe all the red tape we had to go through just to see the man. He agreed to talk to us. We met at a table in the dining hall.

We introduced ourselves and told him why we were here. At first, Swing was hesitant to talk, but when I told him I was prior service, he was willing to talk about Alice. He said, "Man, they tried to hang her death on me, but I was in here. I don't know what knocked her out. The only thing we argued about was the price of a blow job. She said ten instead of five because I didn't want to rear a rubber. Other than that, I had no beef with her. She gave great head."

"Swing, you do know something about all the young women disappearing?"

"Maybe, what's it worth to you?" I slipped him a Grant.

He said, "And his brother Franklin. Ok, you didn't hear this from me. There is a bunch of white fat cats in Brooklyn, selling these women at auction. That's all I know. Come on, give me an address. It moves around. I got a Franklin for every solid lead. Then I had to go and get drunk and start running my big mouth. I Baker acted myself to get thrown in here. I do a little shuffle, and I get free meds, three shots, and a cot. Just like with Uncle Sam. If I go back out there, they will find me."

"Swing, the address!"

"Like I said, they move around. The only place I know of is two blocks down from the nineteenth precinct. Big brick building, I don't know the address. They auctioned off close to 70 women that night. These girls are not just coming from Central Park. Some of these chicks were going for twenty grand. I'm talking high rollers bidding on these women. They are all insulated. You go after these guys, and you are going to wind up dead or in here with me. So, how does Alice fit into all this? Man, don't you get it? They killed her to send a message to all the other bark bums. Keep your mouth shut, or you will die cold and alone."

"Ok, one more question."

"I want to talk to Mr. Franklin again." I slipped him another hundred.

"Who was your contact, some uniform named McGill. I recognized him from a crime scene about four years ago. It was definitely him. Ok, now, you know the cops are in on it. So, take my advice and get the fuck out of dodge by sundown. I'm done here. Peace."

We left the hospital and found a place to eat and talk. Barney said, "How did I know the cops were in on this? Well, one for sure. I don't know if we really want to tangle with these guys."

"Barney, we have to; it sounds like they are throwing thousands of women into white slavery; we don't have a choice. This is so much bigger than us. We have got to bring these people down. I know it's a case of David vs Goliath, but remember, David won that battle and many others."

At this point, we need to know if Frank is involved as well. I'm sure he is no Boy Scout, but he's not a vice detective. Why would they need a homicide man? We will have to put a tail on Frank and see what we come up with. It could reveal more than we want to know.

Back at the hotel room we laid out a flowchart of everything we learned so far, which isn't much. Barney, "Who took Swings place as recruiter in the park?"

He said, "I don't know, but I will try and find out," as he walked out and closed the door.

We know one cop is involved. We suspect that more are involved. From what Swing told us, is looks to involve hundreds of girls. It's a good bet Alice was eliminated because of what she knew.

"Candy, you and I are going to move to a hotel with a better view."

The Eastman Hotel is perfect. From twenty floors up on the park side, we can spy half the landscape. It sucks that room is going to be $500.00 a night. I am sure we can find some way to get our money's worth. "Ok, Billy, let's go. Just tell yourself it's only money."

"Sure, there goes our summer vacation budget. Today is Thursday. We fly back home on Saturday. I was hoping we would be further along than this. We have obligations at home. Call Barney and see if he wants to go home with us."

"Bill, there's no answer."

"Leave a message."

We never heard back from Barney before boarding our plane to New Orleans. I was a little concerned but not totally shocked by this circumstance. He had broken off contact before. He could have at least tried to catch up with us at the hotel. I had hoped to at least get a letter from him.

Several weeks later, on a warm Saturday afternoon, there was a knock at our front door. I opened the door, and Frank Breen was standing there. I said, "Hello."

He asked me if he could come in. I said, "Of course. Sit down and have some freshly made pink lemonade."

"Thank you, Candy."

"What brings you all the way from NYC?"

"Barney is dead! How? When? Frank said they fished him out of the East River five days ago. Someone put two 9mm slugs in him right behind the ear. Ballistics confirmed it was the same gun used in a drive-by five years ago. We think it was a hit. Somebody wanted him dead really bad and in a hurry. This was very sloppy. Usually, a murder like this leaves no forensic evidence whatsoever. Somebody killed Barney with the wrong gun. When was the last time you saw him? I told Frank two days before we flew back home. We tried to call him that evening, but he didn't answer his phone."

Frank said that hotel surveillance had confirmed that he left your hotel alive that afternoon. I was hoping you had seen him after. We are still trying to put the pieces together.

"No, I was a little concerned that he did not call back later. I figured he had money problems and couldn't afford air time on his phone. Money burned a big hole in his pocket. He liked to drink up his SSD check. Damn, I have a hunch it has something to do with the disappearing women."

Frank agreed.

I brought Frank up to speed on what Swing told us.

"Swing isn't telling anyone anything anymore. He committed suicide in his cell a week ago."

I said, "That was very convenient timing, don't you think?"

Frank nodded.

I asked, "What about Officer McGill? Young, ambitious, and fairly well-connected in the department, eventually, he will be my boss if I last that long."

"McGill is small potatoes in this. There have been rumors for years about an underground white slavery operation, but I have never seen anything. Besides, that's vice; they handle prostitution."

"Frank, why did you come all the way out here? We could have done this on the phone."

"Billy, I'm here in person to ask you, as a favor to me, don't pursue this anymore. Barney and Swing Low are both dead. Just let it go.

"Ok, Frank, we will let it go if you answer me one question."

"Ok, shoot."

"Who really sent you here? Billy, I can't tell you that even if I wanted to."

"Alright, have a safe flight back to NYC. I didn't know for sure if Frank was involved until that very moment."

So, some things never change, and the politicians, power brokers, and one-percenters really do call all the shots. It still pisses me off to no end. It's times like this when I really question where God is in all this chaos. Once again, I humbly pray to you, almighty Father. I know that you hear all prayers, and the answers are not based on the needs of the individual.

It's never been about me. I know that. I tell myself that, but this time, God, couldn't it be about me? I don't ask for myself; there are thousands of lives being affected by the culprits committing these acts of kidnapping and sex trafficking. I beseech thy grand mercy for the suffering and anguish these women endure daily. Their lives are not their own, malnourished, constant physical and verbal abuses; how can this repugnant behavior glorify your kingdom? I know it is not my place to ask why. Forgive me, but this day, I am asking why. How can an unspeakable act that goes unnoticed bring about lasting change in my lifetime? God, I feel this situation will not rectify itself during my presence on earth. I have faith. It is the only thing that is pure in its original form. I believe that some good will come about through Alice's death. Maybe Alice had to die in order for me to be with Candy. God, thank you for life, love, and the opportunity to help others in their struggle to find hope in the world. Please watch over my family, my friends, and especially my enemies. Help them to see that loving thy neighbor as thyself is the greatest gift we can give to one another. Amen.

I had already written my sermon for next Sunday. The power of forgiveness. People are somewhat confused and indifferent to forgiving their enemies, and especially praying for them. We all have to remember that we don't necessarily have to like someone to pray for their salvation. My dutiful secretary, Genevieve, informed me that Mrs. Deloach has been waiting to see me. Winifred Deloach is, without a doubt, the biggest busybody in the history of backyard gossip chain busybodies. Lord, give me strength. "Ok, Gina, give me a couple of minutes and send her into my office."

"Good morning, Winifred; how are you doing this beautiful and pastoral day?"

"Well, Reverend, not so good; my neighbor, Wendy Tillis, is up to her old tricks again."

"Is her dog messing up your yard again?"

"Oh yes, and now the little nuisance has taken to crapping and urinating on my hedges. It isn't enough that he digs up my grass to lay around all day; now, he is marking his territory."

"Well," I said, "So talking to her about it does nothing? Ok, you need to go out and get yourself a bigger dog than hers. Make sure it is a pure breed that has not been fixed."

"Hold on, Reverend. You are suggesting that I get a dog myself. Then, I will have two dogs to contend with. No way! In that case, spray something on your lawn to keep the dog from coming over or invest in a fence. A fence! Oh my, no! I can't afford that. I'm on a fixed income. Hold on, Winifred, judging from the generous amount of your tithe every week, I'm confident you can manage to put up some kind of fence. Fine, I see you are going to be no help in this matter. Good day to you, Pastor."

"And to you as well, Mrs. Deloach. Thank you for coming by." In a very murmured voice, I uttered, don't walk under any ladders or break a mirror on the way home. "Lord, give me patience and understanding," I sighed.

"Right now, it would be very convenient," Gina remarked; I heard that. Now, where was I? Oh yes, my sermon on forgiveness. I will dedicate it to Mrs. Deloach. Sunday morning at 11:25 sharp, I began to orate: Friends,

welcome to God's house. Today, I want to speak to you about the rewards of forgiveness. First of all, it'll get you into heaven. That's an easy one. The hard part is softening our hearts in the face of our enemies. When we have the strength to put aside our regret, angst, jealousy, and bile toward another, the healing begins. All of the manufactured hatred we build up within ourselves slowly disappears. Our relationship with the almighty Father is restored. Hearts are softer; souls are cleansed. The fear and anguish are gone. All that remains is clarity and loving-kindness. Sounds great, doesn't it? Your conscience is clear. You no longer reside in Satan's den of inequity. Freedom to love, cherish, appreciate, and live without sin.

One thing remains: you must forgive yourself for your trespasses. Just as we pray for God to forgive us our trespasses, we must be willing to open our hearts and atone for our sinful past. Then, move forward, vowing not to repeat our incredulous mistakes. If you truly find empathy for your fellow man, forgiveness will come pouring out of you. Someone cuts you off in traffic on the way to church so they don't run into you. If they run into your car. It can be fixed.

Racing to anger is always a mistake. God tests us in many ways. It is our ability to stay in control and be slow to anger, Psalms 145, that brings us closer to the Father. Controlling one's anger requires that you recognize stressful encounters as they happen. Not always an easy thing to do. Our emotions can sometimes get the best of us and put us in very compromising situations. Remember, it's not about me, or us for that matter. Just remember that forgiveness is not a sign of weakness. It's a sign of maturity. Becoming enraged during a stressful situation does two things. It prolongs the argument, and it gives your adversary the advantage. Don't lose your head; stay cool and in control. Going on a rant may feel good; after it's over, you are right back where you started. Give your rage to God; you will be one step closer to heaven. Let us Pray.

I exited the front of the church and did all the meet and greets like I always do. After the last cottontop shook my hand, I walked down to the mailbox to gather Saturday's mail. I opened the box, removed the contents, and closed the lid. Just as I pivoted to turn around, a big black SUV came screaming through the parking lot. Shots rang out. I was hit! I fell to the ground, covered in my own blood. Then everything got hazy, and I fell asleep.

Chapter 9: Hide in Plain Sight

I woke up in the hospital, disoriented and paranoid. How did I get here? I tried to move, and every part of my body hurt. I yelled, Help! A nurse came running in the room.

"Mr. Shaw, calm down, or you will rip out all of your staples, the nurse exclaimed."

Then a doctor, I assume he was a doctor, wearing a lab coat and looking mildly important, walked in and proceeded to tell me if it wasn't for him, I would be dead right now.

"Ok, thank you for saving my life; now, would you tell me who, what, when, where, why, and how I got here? The last thing I remember was lying in a pool of my own blood and passing out."

"Ok, Billy, can I call you Billy?"

"Sure, Doc."

The doctor told me, "I had been in an induced coma for two weeks. Candy was on her way here as we spoke. He continued, the police have no idea who shot you 6 times. Two in the right leg, one in the right arm, one severed your right collarbone, and two near your heart. One of which just missed your aorta. You are a very lucky man. Your recovery shouldn't take more than another week or two if you take it easy. I will be by to check on you in a couple of days unless your condition changes. Oh, the police recommended that you take police protection while you are here. That's completely up to you."

"Thanks, Doc, for everything." He walked out, and the nurse came in and changed my bedpan.

Candy showed up about ten minutes later. I asked her how many people knew where I was. She said that she didn't know. It didn't take six bullets to convince me that someone in NYC wants me dead. I can't go to the police. It's pretty obvious that the person or people pulling the strings in that sex trafficking ordeal are covering their tracks. I told Candy we needed to disappear for a while. How about we go camping in upstate New York in a few weeks? Candy agreed.

I was discharged after a pretty routine recovery, considering all the lead I had just eaten. The police were useless. They said the vehicle was stolen and found half submerged down an old swamp road. No prints; it was definitely a professional job. Ok, so why am I still alive? I'm not much of a loose end, but as long as I'm alive knowing what I know, the guys behind this are vulnerable. I think this is a case of needing to hide in plain sight. So off to New York, we go.

It's fall and the Catskills are beautiful this time of year. If we pitch a tent and pay for everything with cash, that should keep us off the grid. No cell phones or computers. Candy wasn't happy about that. We'll never get gas in the same place twice in a row. Same way with buying groceries. The vehicle will be a problem. Texas plates. The truck would have to stay at the campground almost all the time. We would have to use public transportation in and out of NYC. It would be too risky to rent a vehicle. Credit cards can be traced way too easily. Once we arrive in New York, we are going to have to find an honest broker in this deal. Maybe the FBI would be interested in this kind of case. If the women were being transported across state lines, then they should have jurisdiction. Oh shit, Marty Wilson, my old platoon Sgt. His son is in the FBI. Junior is a station chief in Ohio. Marty said he was a real boy scout (straight arrow); I guess we will be going to NY by way of Akron.

Ohio is an interesting state, round on both ends and high in the middle. O-HI-O. Well, more of an arch on both ends. Lots of history. The Ohio Valley region was a hotbed of colonialism in the eighteenth century. Maybe Marty Jr. can elaborate. Candy and I found the Akron FBI field office. It was nestled between an all-night diner on one side and a laundromat on the other. You just have to love the Midwest. Junior was away from the office when we arrived, so Candy suggested we wait over at the diner and maybe get a bite to eat. The apple pie was awesome, of course. I was just scraping the last bite of apple pie off my plate when Jr. walked in. He sat down and ordered a burger and a wedge of apple pie. Jr. said it was the best in the city. I told him I had no complaints. Then he asked me, "Ok, Billy, what are you doing in Ohio, and why all the cloak and dagger stuff? What the hell is going on?"

I said, "Somebody in New York wants me dead. I managed to survive a very convincing drive-by about 2 months ago. There is a big group of human traffickers working in New York City. They killed two of my friends and another acquaintance before coming after me. We're certain the NYPD vice squad and members of Manhattan's nineteenth precinct are in on it. There may be more cops involved. The operation is definitely being protected by law enforcement at a fairly significant level. These people are auctioning off hundreds of sixteen to thirty-year-old women every month. Do you know anything about this at all?"

Jr. said, "Look, all I ever hear about is a bunch of unsubstantiated rumors and innuendo. Nobody knows anything and can prove less. I will tell you this. My first assignment, right out of Quantico, was in Schenectady, New York. We saw lots of women go missing without a trace, but these girls were prostitutes and runaways. Nobody gave a shit. No ransom demand, no FBI. You have hard evidence of the NYPD being involved?"

I said, "Yes! We had an eyewitness. He conveniently hung himself in Belleview Hospital. Two weeks prior, he told us everything he knew. It took a few Franklins to loosen his tongue, but his story sounded very credible. Swing Low, that was his name, got $100.00 for every homeless girl he pointed out living in Central Park. Some dudes would show up in a van and snatch her and all her belongings. It looked like the girls had just packed up and moved on. It's an almost perfect caper. The victims are all but forgotten anyway, so nobody is going to go looking for them. I suspect that my good friend, Alice, saw something she wasn't supposed to, and it got her killed. She was too old for the sex trade, so they knocked her unconscious, stripped her, and let the near-zero temperature that night do the rest. At first, I thought Swing Low killed her because the next time I saw him, he was wearing her favorite scarf. Now, I think he really did find it somewhere. I'm convinced Alice was killed to keep the other homeless in the park from saying anything. I have the address of a building where one of the auctions took place and the vice cop's name, McGill. That's all I got from Swing Low."

Jr. said, "Well, it's pretty thin. You got hearsay from a dead guy. An unsolved murder and a live victim of a drive-by halfway across the country. That's really thin, my friend. I suggest you go home and go into police custody until they find out who tried to kill you. You aren't going to do that, are you?"

I asked Jr., "Is there anyone high up in the Bureau that you trust?"

Jr. reluctantly said, "Yes, one of my instructors at the Academy might be able to help you. It's a long shot, but I will reach out to him. We frequently correspond with him, and I will make a phone call, but not here. Meet me at this address tonight. I will call you when I'm ready."

Candy and I left and found a nice hotel with a king-size vibrating bed. The vibrator only took credit cards. Rats!

Jr. called at the past eleven, so we proceeded to meet him at the appointed location. I pulled the car up next to his, and he said, "My friend at Quantico was aware of a major sting operation in place to nail the ring leaders in this caper. He also told me that his friend, Agent Gardner, was part of the research team doing some of the forensics on the case. At this point, they still don't know how the money is being laundered. Once they establish a paper trail for the transactions, then the New York Office will have them all by the short hairs."

I said, "Ok, how can we help?"

Jr. told me in no uncertain terms to stay out of it and let them handle this. "Billy," he said, "I took a big risk telling you this. Now don't fuck it up for me. If any of our conversations got out, we could all end up dead."

"Look, Jr.," I said, "I'm still a victim here. They want me out of the way. What if I went and told them I wanted in on the deal? I could tell them that Louisiana is the perfect place to embark on a marine vehicle headed for the Caribbean, and I just happened to own six hundred feet of isolated shoreline. Nothing but snakes and gators everywhere. They might be interested. They're probably going to attempt to eliminate me again. If I get word to Officer McGill that I have information about a sting operation. They might be interested. Or he might just shoot me if he finds me first. I think my odds are better if I play my hand out in the open. Also, I have a backup in the form of Candy Oakley here. She can drive tacks with that .357 magnum of hers. That's better than me, and I can empty my 1911 into a playing card at 20 paces."

"Ok," said Jr., "Say I can get Internal Affairs to get McGill to play ball with us. How do you intend to infiltrate that syndicate and manage to stay alive?"

I said, "Simple. I shoot McGill and take his place. Look, McGill is obviously the muscle in this. If there's any killing to be done, who better to do it than a cop? He would be in a position to make any problems go away. He is the key to penetrating their organization. You get IAD to pick up McGill in that Irish watering hole downtown and put the squeeze on him to work with us. We stage his shooting in a public place. He goes into witness protection, and I get an established cover. Win! Win! I come in as an honest broker, another cop who saw an opportunity. My appearance will be disguised. They won't recognize me without my beard and jet-black hair. Meet Det. Sgt. O'Reilly, who recently transferred from the state police for suspicion of corruption. I know this is a little over the top, using me as the inside man, but honestly, I need another identity anyway. I have to die in order in order to keep on living. I have had Army intelligence training. Get your people to check me out. Also, my super sniper wife will be my backup."

Jr. asked, "How good is your wife?"

I said, "Put it this way, she dropped an Elk on the move in the Colorado Rockies at over 800 yards when she was sixteen. I'm an excellent marksman with a pistol, but with a rifle, 200 yds. It is my limit. She's a whole lot better with any firearm of any caliber. Take Candy to the range, but only if your manhood can take it. She can hit a six-inch gong every time at 500 yds. It's damn impressive."

"Ok," he said, "I will take you at your word on that. I don't think my ego could survive it."

Jr. agreed to reach out to his friend Gardner. In the meantime, I would just have to wait it out. The thing that concerned me the most about this whole deal was the number of participants. NYPD, Internal Affairs, FBI, and the Mark, that's a lot of cooks in the kitchen. Somebody is bound to spit in the bouillabaisse at some point. I just hoped that the trap could be set quickly. Now, all I had to do was go back home and figure out how Reverend William Shaw would meet an early demise.

My congregation has been completely beside themselves over the drive-by shooting. I don't think very many people believed the rival gang theory that I was involved in trying to get one of their pregnant female gang members out for good. I had to tell the local police something. They bought it, though. There was a young pregnant African American girl found dead a couple of weeks earlier. I hated using her like that, but I couldn't tell the local PD I was caught up in some NY conspiracy. They would haul me in for observation.

Candy had a good idea of how I could be killed off. It could be an aneurysm brought on by the induced coma I was in for so long. It made sense. I could just die in my sleep. My family doctor could take off the death certificate, and then the coroner would not have to be involved.

Regardless of how Reverend William Shaw was going to die, on paper at least. Candy would play the part of the grieving widow. We agreed not to have any contact whatsoever until this mess was over. It could take a year or more. If that is the cost for me, so be it because I am boarding a private Leer Jet to Quantico, Virginia. It will be basic training all over again. Pushups, sit-ups, and a three-mile run every morning. Thank the good Lord. I quit smoking years ago.

I got off the plane and met my personal instructor, Allen. This guy was not born with a sense of humor. My old drill sergeants from Basic had more personality than this guy. This dude was mental. I have to give him credit, though. The man knew how to survive in any situation. The first phase was Spy 101. Basically, how to be in complete control of one's surroundings while remaining virtually invisible to the people around you. It's not an easy thing to pull off. Definitely, a heightened sense of awareness for me. Then came hand-to-hand combat. That meant weapons and martial arts training. I thought I was a great marksman. What I could do at ten yards, they could do at fifty yards. I learned fast where my mistakes were. Now I was hitting a six-inch gong at 300 yards every time with a 30-06 caliber rifle and cutting a playing card in half at

25 yards with a .45 caliber pistol. My concealed carry piece was a .380 pistol. I was in the ten-ring at 25 yds as well.

Martial arts training was something quite different. I didn't know a snap kick from a roundhouse when I started. By the end of six weeks, I could at least keep myself out of harm's way. Honestly, it wasn't really enough time to turn me into a black belt anyway. I think the best advice my instructor taught me was to run first until cornered, then and only then, fight your way out of a jam.

There was a great deal to learn in the classroom. I had to know and understand FBI procedures and protocols. Boooring, with three o's. Well, I had to learn it anyway. I had to thank them for getting me in the best shape I had ever been in. If I live through this ordeal, Candy is going to love my new six-pack. I miss her terribly, especially at night. We were just out of newlyweds when this came up. She deserved an Academy Award during my staged death scene. I faked a brain aneurism, supposedly brought on by the shooting. The ambulance and funeral parlor actions were carefully overseen by undercover FBI agents. It went off without a hitch. An empty closed casket funeral due to my organ donor status. No questions asked.

Chapter 10: Detective Seargent Hastings

So, Billy Shaw was dead, and Greg Duncan Hastings was alive and kicking. Really, Duncan, what a fucked up middle name. They liked the police detective idea that I had. So, we went with that. I was a ten-year veteran from the Schenectady undercover division. It was the perfect cover, even though Schenectady PD had never even seen me. My transfer to NYPD was due to an allegation of corruption by the FBI. No charges were ever filed for lack of sufficient evidence.

I reported to my new boss on a bright and early Monday morning and proceeded to get balled out by my new boss, Captain Dorsen of the 19th precinct in Manhattan. He assigned me to vice. That was where they needed a new man, and they got me. Dorson was a real hard ass. He told me if I did anything to embarrass Him, the department, the NYPD, and anyone walking by the building that morning, I would be scraping mud off parking meters until he got tired of watching me. I understood perfectly. He introduced me to my new partner, Det. Sgt. McGill. The feds had not stung him yet. The plan was to get both of us in the act of a felony and get McGill to help me infiltrate the syndicate he was working for. McGill gets a new identity when I kill him, and I take his place.

It was going to take time to get this guy used to me. He loved hanging out at that bar he took Candy to last year. The guy really liked the booze. I felt sorry for the lush, always drinking away the memories of two failed marriages. The first wife, Denise, stabbed him with a knife. He was lucky it didn't penetrate all the way through the rib cage, or he wouldn't be here. She thought he was fooling around with her, and she was right. Enter wife #2, Bonnie. She would eventually screw around on him. I guess it's true turnabout is fair play. I told him I could sympathize, and I told him how I was never able to have a relationship with Alice. I changed her name to Mary. I told him she would have been my first wife if we had ever gotten married. I also told Bruce, his first name, about Lena, and he was very attentive to her story. She was such a wildcat I did not have to embellish at all. Of course, he loved the part about how the sheets would crawl up my ass. On one ever forgets the first partner they lay with. Not everyone gets to experience what I did with Lena, though. I never would have been able to share the incredible intimacy I have with Candy if Lena had not been in my life. I thank her so much for that.

Bruce, on the other hand, never really learned how to give in a relationship. Financially, yes, but not the other stuff. Financial security is extremely important in a marriage. By itself, it is never enough. Trust, respect, and sexual awareness have to be there as well. You can never take your spouse for granted. Please and thank you go a long way to establishing intimacy in a long-term relationship. It is the here and now, that is what makes or breaks an intimate moment between lovers. The ability to convey a sense of true tenderness before you even start foreplay. What it comes down to is taking out the trash, then washing and putting away the dishes. That took me way too long to learn. I think I was actually starting to get through to Bruce. He seemed genuinely interested in listening to all my bullshit. After that, I just sat at the bar, nursed my double scotch on the rocks for a while, and listened to everything that Bruce had to say.

He had such expectations of himself right out of the academy, like everyone else in the dept. Took a fast track to try and make a Detective in under five years. Night classes, special assignments, etc., helped to move his career along. Also, he had a relative downtown to give him a boost in the right direction every now and then. He kept telling me that it was a good idea to try and make friends with all the right people. Especially someone with my rather unique background as a detective. I think he was eluding to my alleged corruption charge. Man, they don't waste any time. I've been here less than a week and they are already feeling me out to see which side of the fence I'm on. I told him that the prevailing winds would usually carry me in the direction that I needed to follow. I find that it is not good to make waves. A calm sea is always much easier to navigate. Being an ex-navy man, he liked the ocean metaphors. I felt very strongly that it would not be long before I would be knee-deep in some really nasty scheme.

My contact at the Bureau was Smith. I was to contact him with a burner phone every 72 to 96 hrs. If I did not, it meant my cover was blown, or I was dead. Quid pro quo, if I did not hear back in 24 hrs., then I knew my cover was blown on their end, and I had special instructions on how to get back home to Mother. I checked in on time and met with Smith at the appointed time and place. We exchanged situation reports and went on our separate merry little ways. My instructions were to keep feeding them intel until I knew who McGill was working for. Smith said not to rush anything. Just let every opportunity unfold naturally. Slow and steady will get to the prize.

Bruce and I were back at the precinct the next morning, trying to look busy. I'm sorry, but Bruce always had a disheveled look about him. A very staunch fellow, fairly handsome, but so surly around the edges. Like someone who had too much high-octane coffee after a hangover. That was Sgt. McGill. My new partner for life, it seemed. After a week with the man, already his boorish demeanor was weighing on me heavily. Bruce came out of the captain's office and headed down the stairs. I was learning quickly that if I wanted to stay up on everything, I had to move quickly. So, out the door right behind him, I went. Bruce said, "We are going on a little errand for the C.O."

"Where to?"

"Don't worry about that. Just keep your mouth shut and follow my lead. We are going to speak with one of the captain's snitches."

"Ok."

Bruce drove us to the address where Swing Low told me the slave auction was held. We pulled up to the delivery entrance, and Bruce honked loudly three times. The bay door slowly opened. We rolled in and parked in the closest space to a small office. The rest of the warehouse was filled with metal shipping containers. It was odd that they all had a window and a wall air conditioner on one side. Bruce introduced me to Mr. Smith. I said, "Hello."

"Call me Robert."

"Why do all these shipping containers have air conditioners attached to them?"

"Good question, Greg." He opened one of the doors to one of the containers, and there was a beautiful half-naked woman sitting on a lounge chair. She stood up and walked toward me. Then she said, "I'm Deseree. Are you next?"

"Next for what?"

"You came here for a fuck, right?"

"No, I guess I'm a little confused." She walked back to the chair and sat down.

Then Robert yelled, "I thought you said this guy was one of us?"

Bruce said, "He is; this is his first time here."

"Oh, ok, Greg, get your ass in the box. Then stick your dick in her box, so we can film you doing it. Ok."

"And if I refuse?"

Robert walked over to me, put his arm on my shoulder, and said, "Look, either that or several of these gentlemen holding firearms are going to hang you up by your neck until you are dead."

"Can I use a condom?"

"Sure, but you got to pull it off for the money shot."

"Will do."

This was my initiation into their syndicate. They would always have videos of me to use as blackmail. How the hell am I going to explain this one to Candy? I guess I will have to figure that one out later. One thing was abundantly clear: if I gave any appearance like I was tied into some sort of sting operation, I would end up dead, and my reputation would be destroyed. I got to hand it to them. That's one way to keep people from talking. I will bet Smith doesn't even know about this stuff. I'm in that's the important thing. Looks like I'm up to my neck. After my spectacle with Deseree, who was very good, she made sure that I was comfortable and not camera shy in any way. She made a very awkward moment plausible for me. She kept whispering in my ear that I was doing great. I just had to keep going a little longer. I'm really glad that it's over and done with. Now, I really want to nail these guys.

When Bruce and I got back to the car, he let me in on the deal. I would be part of Robert's private security team. Also, we all received our bribe money on camera. These bastards didn't miss a trick. The next auction was in two weeks at another location.

I asked, "How long has this thing been going on?"

"I heard approximately ten years. Look, don't ask any questions, and make damn sure you always show up on time. Not every vice cop is in on this. The reason you were recruited is because of your misgivings with I.A.D. Otherwise, you would be out driving a paddy wagon three times a week or scraping mud off parking meters. It's not a bad gig, even if it does make you a dirty cop. You get paid at the end of every Job. $200.00 an hour to start. It goes up from there. You earn your money, though! Some of these rich, fat cat customers don't always know how to behave themselves. You wouldn't believe some of the big-name celebrities who get off on this stuff. And boy, do they get off. On the pillow, the carpet, the walls, everywhere."

"You said auction?"

"Yes, the girls get auctioned off to the highest bidder. I have seen Deseree go for over $100,000. That was a wild night; most of the really good ones go for between $10,000 to $20,000. Others go for as little as $1000."

"You're telling me I just had sex with a $100,000 prostitute?"

"Yeah, but they're mostly doing it against their will. I don't think prostitution is really a fair way to describe them. Personally, I would consider them more as a private harem. They aren't permitted to go anywhere in public for at least a year. Honestly, it's nothing more than white slavery, just at a whole lot higher level. Some of these girls, like Deseree, are recruited. Then there are the wildcats that they get off the street. Sometimes they work out, and sometimes they don't. That's when we earn our money after a killing."

"How often does that happen?"

"Not often. Every few months. That's really all you need to know. Like I said, show up on time, and as long as you don't get nosy, you will be fine. Other than that, just enjoy the money. One other thing: no big luxury items. Boats, sports cars, expensive jewelry, expensive girlfriends, and real estate are not on the menu. Moderation is the key to staying alive around here. Look, max out your payroll investing, and drive a late-model car; nobody will get wise to you. Pretty soon, you will be off your ninety-day probation, and I.A.D. will think that you are invisible. Then you can live a little."

"Ok, I can do that."

"Good, now, let's go get something to eat."

I never saw an Irishman eat so much Italian food in one sitting. I busted a gut just watching him. We went to this little mom-and-pop place just outside Manhattan called *Mama Royale.* Strange name, incredible food. Checkered tablecloths, the whole package. Of course, they sold pizza, too. I ordered the Shrimp Scampi, probably the best I had ever eaten. The table wine was awesome. I would be coming back there, for sure. For takeout, at least.

This gig is starting to drag on a bit. I haven't seen or talked to Candy in almost four months. I have to keep telling myself that it's really not about me. Even when I was forced to have intercourse with Deseree, I just kept telling myself that I was just a player in a larger production. No matter what they ask of me, I can't lose faith. I just hope they don't ask me to kill someone in cold blood.

My apartment is nice. I found a two-bedroom for $1800.00 a month. I thought that was decent. It's only a twenty-minute commute on the Subway. Only one transfer, thank the Lord. So far, I'm adjusting to big city life enough to be credible anyway. I didn't expect to be brought into the fold so quickly. The feds were right, act as though you could really give a shit, and they will throw you right into the mix. Well, they sure did that. They didn't waste much time finding out just how much I would be willing to go along with. I'm not even going to bother getting a vehicle. I just can't justify spending another grand a month just for the privilege of ownership. If I need a vehicle, I can always rent. Screw the insurance, taxes, traffic, parking, and road rage. I can spend the money on something else much more worthwhile. I'm sure I'm not the first cop who didn't own a personal vehicle. The NYPD has plenty of impounded clunkers I can drive around when the need arises. So far, Bruce has done all the driving, which is fine with me. I can scan the horizon and watch all the bums urinate and defecate all over the city. It's a rare treat watching some guy crap on a grassy median, then drag his butt on the ground like some dog with an irritated anus. The sights and sounds of the city. The Big Apple, there's no place like it on earth.

I can empathize with what homeless people have to go through just to survive. Once someone has allowed themselves to slip that far away from what society deems acceptable social behavior, it must be very easy to just let go and live life without any filters. Eventually, one's only personal hygiene takes place during a rain or snowstorm. When I was living in Central Park, I ended up taking a couple of bowel movements in the woods with my old entrenching tool. Luckily, the ground was soft enough to dig a cat hole. It wasn't all that dignified, and I'm sure it was against the law. At least I buried it. Now, when the Therma frost has penetrated twelve inches deep, it is much more difficult. Luckily, NY doesn't get extremely frigid winters. Still, it is challenging digging around here in the dead of winter.

Bathing and shaving were not a huge priority when I was living on the street. I did keep myself clean. I tried not to accumulate too much body odor. It is hard to gauge that. I would look at the people around me and see if my presence repulsed them in any way. Most of the time, I was ok. I don't think anyone suspected I was sleeping outside almost every night. I did manage to get into a shelter one weekend; I was conflicted about that because I considered my being there a waste of resources. As it turns out, my stay there was justified in the fact that I met Alice the first night in the shelter. We hit it off immediately. I think we talked until about 3:00 AM. I still can't quite wrap my head around why she was made to suffer so hard and die in such anguish. I would still like to kick Larry right square in the balls. Make him suffer! Cause him anguish! It's ok, though; at least I'm not bitter about it very much, heh. I do believe wholeheartedly heartily what comes around, goes around. Karma is a bitch when it falls heavy on anyone. Larry has a big dose coming his way eventually. Mother Nature has a way of keeping us in line. When I was in my twenties, I could drink and smoke all night, crash four or five hours, and get up the next morning fresh as a daisy. Once I turned thirty, that flower was a shriveled-up mess after a night of partying. A few drinks around dinnertime is more my speed. I've never really been a heavy boozer. I guess because of what it did to my folks. I'm thirty-two, and they're both gone. I will never condone their lifestyle choices, but I thank them for having me.

Chapter 11: I am in Deep

I get a little nervous just hanging around the squad room, waiting for something to happen. I'm not impersonating a homicide detective, thank the maker. So, my skill set doesn't have to be that impressive. One feather in my cap is the fact that I am very good at interacting with people from all walks of life. Being exposed to the homeless firsthand taught me that. I notice that can be a trigger for some of my co-workers who don't possess that skill. It is a delicate balance between identifying someone who is telling a blatant lie and showing empathy for the reason why they are doing it. Trust and a deep-seated hatred of authority figures cause many people to see public safety as a mortal enemy. The Police, Government, etc., are not the real enemy; poverty is. That's the thing very few people recognize as the largest bane in society. When too many people are forced to share too few resources, i.e., nourishing food, adequate healthcare, affordable housing, and a living wage, it tears at the fabric of an individual's soul until there is nothing left. Then desperation sets in and leads to crime and prejudice on many levels. Law enforcement is not immune by any means. Police, Fire, EMTs, and the like all struggle with knowing when to say when. When do they get to go home and feel good about something that happened earlier at work that day? Maybe when a baby is born or a kid from the project's graduates from college. Those keynote celebrations come along very infrequently. Instead, it's drive-by and funerals.

The Law doesn't care that an elderly woman on a fixed income has to choose between healthy sustenance and pain medication at the end of every month. Schoolchildren only get two meals a day, five days a week. Most are out hustling for a meager meal on weekends. If they are lucky, one of the local churches will feed them on Sunday. The cycle of abuse by their surroundings is damning for many. Society has no use for them. This is why I became a man of the cloth. Broken, Sad, hopeless, and homeless, they need our help, not our pity. I hear the other officer's sneers when I offer comfort to a welfare mother who got caught hooking in the park. I give her a soda or cup of coffee, and they just laugh. I just hope I don't give myself away. I asked one of them in the break room if they had ever been homeless. They said no, of course. I barked, "Uh, huh!" Then I walked out of the room. It didn't change his mind, but I certainly felt better having said it.

Bruce Hung up the phone and yelled to me, "We're on the road." I shot up out of my chair and headed to the motor pool. We got a call from the boss to remove a body. This time, the warehouse was in Queens. A huge building that looked abandoned from the outside. Once inside, more of the same. Shipping containers that had been converted into dorm rooms to accommodate clients. It was amazing how immaculate these accommodations were. Mirrored ceilings, S&M accessories, and fully stocked liquor cabinets. The interiors rivaled luxury hotel rooms. The women were all just breathtaking. It was like I walked into the lobby of a modeling agency. Every nationality is represented.

We finally got to the dead girl's body. Judging from the ligature marks, she choked to death, probably during a sex act. We filled the body bag and headed for Harlem. Another big warehouse, this time it was empty. Only half of the parking garage was concrete. Bruce backed the unmarked vehicle almost to the edge of the concrete slab and tossed the body in the dirt. The two portable cement mixers did the rest. As we drove away, I thought to myself, this is incredible. If I don't expose this illegal cemetery, No one will ever know anything. It's appalling, but I have to be impressed at the entire operation. This is a multi-million-dollar business being executed blocks from a police station. The world's oldest profession is now a playground for one-percenters. They even have a fully staffed clinic to deal with anything from STDs to medical emergencies.

Bruce said as we were driving back to the station, "You just made $2500.00, my friend. That ain't bad for two hours of work. There's an auction party on Monday night. You need to get to the Queen's warehouse at 8:45 pm sharp. Like I said before, do not be late. Now, let's get something to eat."

"Ok."

For a moment, I thought to myself, the hell with the feds, man, this is paradise. They have thought of everything. Then, half a minute later, I regained my senses and condemned the entire scheme. When I report back to Smith, he is going to freak. I think the best way to nail these guys would be to get them all for murder. I'm sure that the warehouse basement in Harlem must be full of bodies. I doubt it will be easy to connect that building to whoever is behind all this. They have got to be insulated very well. That's for the forensics boys to figure out, not me. It is scary how they can tie somebody up so badly electronically. Me, I'm playing it cool and keeping my big mouth shut. That's what they seem to appreciate around here. Don't try to be a hero. Hopefully, that will come much later.

I was right. Smith freaked when I told him that I helped Bruce dispose of a dead sex worker's body. He agreed with me that tying the syndicate to that was going to be tough. He did say that my affidavit would probably be enough for a wiretap on Bruce. In order to get any evidence in this case, the Feds. Would have to flip McGill. It would be difficult for me because I kind of like the guy. I know he was up to his elbows in conspiracy charges, but I think he was trapped in this the same way I was. I'm sure there's a sex DVD of him somewhere. Maybe even more than one. We are still fishing at this point. Now, at least, we know where these women are ending up. All a raid would do know is to cause the auction parties to relocate. Plus, it would surely blow my cover. That would not do anyone any good. I should know more after I work for the auction party. I wonder what I will be doing there. Anything from parking lot detail to bartending. Who knows. I just have to wait and see.

Monday evening arrived. I showed up exactly when I was supposed to, along with six other gentlemen. Three of them were fellow officers from my precinct. The bay door opened, and we walked inside to the freight elevator and took a ride to the third floor. It was a ballroom lavishly decorated. $20,000 chandeliers, the tables were decorated with gold-trimmed chargers surrounded by a ten-piece place setting. It resembled a White House State dinner. A huge dancefloor, with a twelve-piece jazz ensemble playing. Four Steamship round buffets, caviar, shrimp cocktail, baked Alaska, etc. Holy shit. Then, in came the guests. There must have been a hundred well-dressed gentlemen scurrying to find their place cards after everyone was seated. The band leader announced dinner was served. The auction will start in exactly one hour. Bon appetite.

As dinner came to a close, the band leader rose to introduce the Emcee for the evening none other than Captain Dorsen. The first girl, a leggy blonde, went for $18,000. This went on for quite a while. Girls went for as much as $45.000. Some of these men bought three and four women for the evening. I stood at my security post and said nothing unless I was spoken to. Talk about Sodam and Gamora. I found out later that night the entry fee to this little shindig was $25,000. This place had it all. It even had a drug bar. Coke, hash, grass, whatever you wanted. I did notice a few faces in the crowd. Most notably, Senator Reynolds, an ordained minister like me. He bought two women for the evening. At precisely 11 pm, several grandfather clocks rang out, and everyone headed to the elevators to take a short ride down to the basement and round out the evening festivities. Security personnel took the stairs. Then, we stood guard as our honored guests did what they paid for the privilege to do. Some six hours later, the men appeared fully dressed outside of the storage containers and departed. Security went to the second floor, where all the guests waited for their prearranged exit. Nothing was left to chance. If I didn't know any better, I would swear it was just another work day in downtown Manhattan.

At the end of the week, when I reported to Smith, he was impressed. We both knew that Capt. Dorsen would have to be turned. So, another wiretap. I did not see that one coming. Dorsen stood up there and sold those women off like a professional livestock auctioneer. He had to have gone to auctioneer school.

I didn't know how they planned to break Dorson down, it turned out to be a good point. He flopped like a pancake. I guess when you are completely compromised, there is nothing to do but go along and hope for the best. My cover was still intact, so I stayed on.

I feel bad for McGill; he is going to fall pretty hard. I can't prove it, but I am guessing that Capt. Dorson cut himself a deal for cooperating. I would love to know what he knows. My weekly meeting with Smith is tonight. So, hopefully, I will get full disclosure.

I walked into the diner where we usually meet, and no Smith. I headed for the secondary location. I pulled into the Connecticut Welcome Center on I-95. There was Smith.

I said, "Hey, why the change in location."

"Just, being cautious. I have plenty to cover today."

"What's up with Dawson?"

"As you may have guessed, Dawson rolled over like one of my wife's meatballs. He gets early retirement due to medical. In exchange for testimony. Turns out there are three men who control the operation. The top guy, even Dawson, doesn't know. There are around sixty, either active or retired NYPD, on the payroll. One auction will bring in anywhere between 1.5 to 2 million dollars per auction. The girls work strictly on gratuity. They do get free wardrobes, meals, and housing. Dawson told me some of those girls make over $5,000 a night. We don't want to arrest the girls. We just want ringleaders.

Any of the police who cooperate get a good report IAD and should end up with just a slap on the wrist. My bosses don't want this to be a media circus, so based on the information given to us by Dawson, arrest and search warrants will be issued sometime next week. We have a copy of the guest list. There are two circuit court judges and one of our men. He's been dealt with. We decided not to do a raid on one of the auction parties. It could turn into a high-profile blood bath. We don't want that. We are going to try and arrest as many of the Johns as we can before they leave the country. Good news for you, your part in this is just about over."

"Cool. When do my wife and I get new identities?"

"About a week after this is all over, you are going to come down with Covid. Nobody will want to follow up with you on that. Then you and Candy will be out of here."

"You still need my testimony, right?"

"Well, we have Dawson, but yes, we need yours to collaborate with his."

"Ok. I will be at the precinct like I always am, waiting for a phone call. Meet back here next week, right?"

"No, back at the diner, I have a weakness for their Apple pie a la mode."

"Ok."

I headed back into the city, grinning from ear to ear; soon, I would be back in Candy's sweet arms again. it has been almost six months since I last saw my love. I don't know whether to cry or scream; I'm so happy right now. Then I thought to myself, easy Bill, I still got another week of this.

Four days later, the warrants were served. Over fifty arrests were made. I wouldn't want to be in Dawson's shoes right now. The FBI confiscated three offices worth of files and computers, mostly purchase orders and campaign contributions. In order to get a guilty verdict, they would need my and Dawson's testimony. Buried underneath that warehouse basement in Harlem were seventy-eight human skeletal remains. All of them were encased in cement. It took over two months to excavate them all.

The bodies were found, and the witnesses were willing to testify, even some of the prostitutes. Where was the money? How do you hide an estimated 300 million dollars? The money was a big problem. Without it they could not tie anything to David Cooke, the big man himself. He is currently living in Vermont, completely insulated from any impropriety in this case. The arrogant bastard is living quite comfortably out in the open knowing full well there is no way to connect him to any of this. Where's the damn money.

Deseree, my muse in all this, remembered hearing one of her johns bragging about something called the vault. He never said where it was but that he had one of three keys that opened it. Apparently, it contained the equivalent of King Solomon's treasure, T-bills, precious gems, gold bullion, stolen artworks, etc. Dawson claimed to know nothing about it. If it was located in NYC, then someone on that private security team knew the whereabouts of that thing. Every building. In Cooke's New York empire, sonar was scanned from head to toe. It had to be in the city. The files were, along with the bodies.

Where do you hide a vault the size of a cargo plane in plain sight? In a bank, of course. There are three financial institutions with multiple vaults. Good luck getting a search warrant for any of them. So far FBI investigators had not been able to locate anything tying those institutions to Cooke. Even the best crew with a month to plan the job couldn't get in and out of that vault, but what if they only had to get in? Hmm.

Chapter 12: Alaska

Alaska is a very cold place, and anyone who says anything to the contrary is full of frozen moose crap. Take it from me: I am a real expert on moose scat at this point. Juneau, Alaska, is the northwest end of civilization. The feds couldn't relocate us to Key West or New Orleans. Oh no, we end up in Sewerd's ice box. Thank you so much for this winter wonderland. There's just one problem. I hate snow!! One thing is for sure: Candy and I are safe. Unless a lost polar bear is working for Paul Duncan, that's the HDIC of the illegal prostitution/sex worker ring. I haven't talked to Smith since being sent to this barren ice cube of a town. At least we can hunt and fish up here. If we could not do that, we would be crawling the walls around here. The nights are ok. I have Candy to cuddle up with. She's a really good cuddler.

I can't believe we are going to be stuck here until the trial. It's on the docket and scheduled for February. That's only ten months away. I'm sure we can lay low until then. Juneau has over 30,000 residents. It's also the state capitol. I have a feeling that is why we ended up here. Where better to hide out than a big municipal tourist town? Blending in here won't be as bad as say, Wainwright, AK. Go to the middle of nowhere and head northeast as far as land will take you; that's Wainwright. It's a small petroleum village. It does have some character. Certainly, there are worse places. Actually, the climate is not as unbearable as one might think. The winters aren't any worse than in northern Minnesota. Burr!

Candy has already landed a job in one of the local beauty salons. I start working with a local food bank, as a warehouse manager next week. The salaries are really good here, but the cost of living is really high. I'm still omnipresent to the fact that it is never about me. People struggle everywhere. Even in a place so rich in natural landscape, commerce and consumerism still find a way to eat away at the souls of the inhabitants here. Major crime, domestic violence, theft, vice offenses, it's all here. All I can do is pray every morning for the strength to make a difference in people's lives every day. One regrettable constant in every city throughout the U. S. is poverty and the need for food security.

Candy came walking through the door on her way home from work, gave me a very passionate kiss, grabbed my ass with both hands, and proceeded to undress me right in front of the stove.

I said, "I'm cooking dinner."

"I want you now!"

I turned off the stove and followed her to the bathroom. We showered and then made love for quite a while. My phone rang, it was Smith.

I answered, "I thought you were not going to call us while we were up here. What is going on?"

"You and Candy have to move right now. Your cover has been compromised. Start packing. A car will be picking you up in an hour. Take nothing but a change of clothes, toiletries, and your identification."

"Ok, but you have a great deal of explaining to do."

As promised, approximately forty-five minutes later, an unmarked vehicle pulled into our driveway. Two ridiculously overdressed dark-haired men wearing dark sunglasses came running up to the door, and one of them shouted, "ok folks, hurry it up; we have a plane to catch."

Candy and I were out the door and on our way to a safe house in Seattle, WA, very quickly. I inquired why we were being expedited so quickly, but there was no answer. So, I let it go. We landed in a small military air base just north of Seattle. Smith was waiting with a vehicle. Once seated in the back of the big black SUV, I shouted, "Smith, what the hell is going on?"

"I am sorry for all the cloak and dagger stuff, but Cooke found out about you and Candy. He sent two mechanics to eliminate you. Their flight just landed in Juneau."

"Well, it is very apparent that you have a very big leak in your department.

"So, where do you plan on hiding us now?"

"At Quantico. You both will be fully disguised, working as archive investigators. We are going to hide you in plain sight and leak a story that you have been flown to Israel and put into protective custody of the Musad. I hope this will flush out the mole that Cooke has in the FBI. I have narrowed it down to three men. Unfortunately, I work for two of them. The other one is me. I swept my vehicle, home, office, and family for any hidden surveillance devices. I am convinced that I have not been compromised. It has to be one of my bosses. My immediate supervisor, a man named Reinhardt, I have known since my academy days. I seriously doubt he has been compromised. His boss, Paul Fisher, is a career boot-licking asshole. I hope to God it turns out to be him."

"How did you find out we were compromised."

"I still had access to Cooke's text messages. He sent a message to a known assassin. Then, Both men were spotted by airport security in Brussels. Another three hours and you would have been dead for real."

"When is the trial?"

"In two months."

"I have a place picked out for you and Candy. You both will be staying at a hotel near Arlington, VA. We have only put a federal witness on ice like this one other time. It proved to be very successful. I am very confident that your whereabouts will not be compromised."

Candy retorted, "I am glad you are confident. It is not your ass in a sling if this all goes to shit."

Smith remarked, "That is true, but who would suspect a couple of nerdy librarians working in the basement of an FBI training facility."

"Honey, he has a valid point."

I quipped, "Free wet bar?"

"I will see what I can do."

We were off to Arlington. We could not even visit the cemetery. Two months of hanging out at the library. Then back to the hotel. Part of our commute is by rail. I love traveling by train, even if it is only for forty minutes a day one way. I never get tired of looking out those giant picture windows. Every day is just a bit different. The leaves are just starting to change. With each commute, the colors get a little stronger. It is God's canvas. I find such resolve in gazing out into the forest of color. Squinting my eyes helps to blend the reds, oranges, and yellows. Candy makes fun of me when I squint out the window. She glares at me, staring at my reflection on the glass. Then we get into a tickle fight. It is fun to be a newlywed.

The library gig is actually kind of cool. Agents from all over call in for information on a wide variety of subject matter. Then there are the trainees, and they can be a handful at times. The day goes by pretty fast. Some days, we barely have time for a ten-minute lunch, consisting of a cold sandwich from the commissary three flights up. Other days we get to eat in the canteen. Once we got to eat in the executive lounge. That was a real treat. The clam chowder was fabulous. Those bureaucrats are a giant pain in the ass most of the time, but they sure do eat well. I guess they felt bad about the breach of security and threw us a bone.

Five days before the trial, Smith and an FBI lawyer named David Morris briefed me on my testimony. It was more of a grilling. They asked me questions about everything. Old girlfriends, Army stuff, and some of it was rather pointless. Like, had I ever had a vasectomy? I never made the connection, but I guess there was one. While I was testifying, Candy would be at an undisclosed military airport waiting onboard a private jet. As far as Candy and I were concerned they had done everything we asked of them and more.

My ride to the courthouse was not nearly as eloquent as the previous rain commutes. I sat in the back of a giant black SUV scrunched between two extra-large FBI bodyguards. One of which forgot his deodorant that morning. Well, at least I had the illusion of being safe and secure. The driver pulled the SUV into the courthouse garage located in the basement. Before they opened the vehicle door, I had to put a hood on to conceal my identity. I did not really see the point. I guess they were just following the procedure. Once we got into the elevator, they removed my hood. Next stop, the eleventh floor. Then we walked down the stairs on two flights. I was immediately taken to a special room to await being called to the witness stand. About ten minutes later, I was escorted to the courtroom and directed to the witness stand.

The prosecutor stood up and introduced himself. Then he began to question me. "Good afternoon, Mr. Shaw. Would you please state your full name for the court."

"William Edward Shaw."

"Mr. Shaw, for the better part of seven months, you worked undercover for the Federal Bureau of Investigation, yes or no?"

"Yes."

"What was your role in the operation?"

"I was placed working as a Detective Sargeant in the Manhattan, New York nineteenth precinct of the NYPD."

"During that time, you were working undercover for the nineteenth precinct. Did you witness, firsthand, any felonious activity perpetrated by any other members of the NYPD?"

"Yes"

"Would you please elaborate for the court?"

"Certainly. On March 10, Captain Dorson ordered Detective McGill and myself to report to a warehouse approximately three blocks due east of the nineteenth precinct building and remove a dead body. It was a young woman approximately twenty to twenty-five years of age. She was completely undressed and had ligature marks completely surrounding her neck. There were also visible bruise marks surrounding her upper arms. Sgt. McGill instructed me to help him load her into a body bag. We then proceeded to carry the corpse to our unmarked police vehicle and drive to an undetermined location in Harlem, New York. After arriving in Harlem, we proceeded to another warehouse. We drove into the basement. McGill backed the car up to the edge of a concrete slab. We exited the vehicle, removed the body from the trunk, and tossed it into an approximately five-foot-deep makeshift grave. There was a gentleman standing next to the edge of the hole. He proceeded to fill the hole with concrete, stopping periodically to lay reinforcing wire in the concrete."

"Your Honor, people exhibit twenty-two. Mr. Shaw, did it appear that this procedure had taken place before?"

"Yes, the entire basement floor had been formed one six by ten concrete slab at a time. I could not count all of them in the time I was there."

"Then what transpired?"

"Sgt. McGill and I got back in our vehicle and returned to the squad room at the nineteenth precinct."

"Do you recall another incident where felonious activity took place?"

"Yes. On March 20, I was part of a security detail on the third floor of the previously mentioned warehouse where I was witness to an auction selling women to the highest bidder."

"Did you recognize the auctioneer?"

"Yes, it was my supervisor, Captain Dawson."

"Your precinct Captain?"

"One and the same, sir."

"No more questions, your honor."

The judge said, "Your witness, counselor."

"No questions, your honor."

"Very well, the witness may exit the courtroom."

Not at all what I expected. I am just glad that all this is behind me now. I can get on with my new life. I got back in the SUV, and we headed for the airport. Candy was waiting diligently for me. We boarded the jet, and Smith was waiting to ask us where we wanted to go. I told him, "Boise, Idaho."

Smith said, "Good choice. You can find work as a clergyman, and Candy can go back to Cosmetology. We will give you new identities, and that, folks, is all she wrote."

"Good. I have had enough excitement to last me quite a while."

"Relax. Well, have to refuel in Kansas City, and the next stop will be Idaho."

I punched down a few double scotch and sodas, then fell asleep.

Chapter 13: Boise

Boise, Idaho, was not what Candy or I expected. An ocean of hunter orange. The trout fishing is amazing, though. I wish the season weren't so short. I am now preaching at a small non-denominational church. The Wisdom of Faith Fellowship of the Holy Tabernacle. It is a mouthful. I call it home now. The people here are wonderful. Very conservative, as one would expect, but kind to a fault. Any visitor who walks through our doors on Sunday morning is showered with love. Our guests are treated like family. At the conclusion of the service, they are cordially invited to dine with the entire congregation, all eighty-seven of us, in the fellowship hall for a delicious Sunday Brunch buffet. Every service I pray we have at least one guest. Two of our members are professionally trained chefs. The omelet bar and Eggs Benedict are out of this world. There is always a profound hush over the congregation when we do not have any visitors.

I now have a new fellowship to grace every Sunday morning. Many kind-hearted people do not seem to know the evil that constantly lies around them. This is definitely by choice. See, no evil, hear no evil is practiced daily around here. Common sense is pretty common around here, even in the local politics. There is a sense of fairness in the decisions made in this part of the country. Granted, everything evolves around the scarcity of natural resources, water, ore, timber, etc., but there is a propensity to give back to the community. Tithes are consistent and very generous at times. Idahoans have not lost respect for themselves or the people around them.

Additionally, we have a Wednesday night fellowship, which is extremely popular with the homeless and low-income families in the area. It can draw as many as 500 diners a week. I suspect many of the individuals who take advantage of our weekly meals are probably not eating a nourishing diet most of the time. Boise is certainly not where I expected to end up at this point in my life, but God's work must be carried on everywhere. I do feel that Candy and I are part of the solution now. I sleep better at night knowing this.

I wish I had been able to do more to help the victims I left in New York City. For my part, it seemed a little too easy. Granted, going undercover as part of the sting operation was intense and risky, but I did not feel that I was in any danger while doing it. I guess my background story must have passed muster. Candy's, as well.

Now, she is working as a hostess for the premier hair salon in Boise. She makes a ton of money now. I have been working as a professional tutor for middle and high school-age students. I love working with young people, but I wish the money were better. I considered teaching high school, but I think it would take too much away from my pastoral responsibilities. I do draw a small gratuity from the congregation. When the church elders initially offered it to me, I turned it down, but they insisted that I take it. I hate to admit it, but most of my congregation is very well off.

Many of them come from much more traditional religious backgrounds. I believe that my inspired message may allow them the opportunity to not feel self-conscious about having wealth. I know that money is the root of all evil, but if it is used in a manner befitting God's plan, then sin is absent. However, there will always be a slippery slope to avoid. Accountability is key in assuring good works are accomplished.

I think back to the decision I made to burn that winning lottery ticket. Some good would have come from that money. That choice may have been made in some haste. I just could not see through the chaos of trying to justify such a decision. Having to delegate over 400 million dollars was just overwhelming. The money was not so much the problem as the bedlam I foresaw that it would create. Money in that amount would create trust issues, skepticism, greed of course, jealousy, etc. A small-town church is just not the venue for such an undertaking. I completely get why the person who sent me the ticket did what they did. I am sure they had to be thinking enough is enough. That individual had to be a retiree. I like to think that had much to do with the decision to forward the winning ticket to me. Why didn't they just give it to some homeless person and be done with it? Guilt weighed very heavily on their decision to pass the burden on to me. I was tested. I pray I made the right decision. Hopefully the lottery office will find a resolution to the unclaimed ticket, which becomes void after one year from the time of purchase anyway.

I never did tell Candy about that incident. Only a handful of people know the existence of that ticket, and as far as I am concerned, the less, the better. If word got out that I had destroyed it, the shitstorm that would arise would be furious. Burning the thing was a simple and practical means to an end. I should do well to recognize it is not in my best interest to second guess decisions from the past. History is constantly being forged moment by moment. There is no changing the past. All I can do is pray and go forward. Lord, I ask forgiveness for the sins I have committed. It is my sincere hope that they do not bring harm to others.

I still cannot push back the feeling that money or wealth is easily corruptible. I never saw that so plain as when I saw the sodomy that transpired in NYC. All those manipulated lives are constantly put into such jeopardy in pursuit of selfish sexual release at the hands of others. Sometimes, just for a moment, I wish that I could step outside my passive role as a man of God and thwart the Godless enemy that would rein evil and vengeful interrogation upon those powerless to smite their enemies. Selfish, most elite men created a world where they could play out their misogynistic fantasies, including the occasional murder, only to satisfy the carnal perversion conjured up by thoughts of unbridled power to rule others. Our current U.S. Constitution does not condone the torture of persons who seek to do evil in the name of personal gratification, but it should. An eye for an eye, a tooth for a tooth, torture for torture. That would be a suitable means to an end.

That would feel so good for a moment or two. The ability to strike back at the heart of one's foes. I could lash out at those who would want to harm me or others I choose to care for. No regret or remorse for my actions. Just evil for evil. Afterall, it is their way of thinking. The nature of man. Conquer or suffer the fate brought upon by your enemies. Fortunately, I have chosen another path.

I will obey the law of the land and seek to find fortune in forgiveness. Striking at one's victim a second time does nothing to the oppressed. It does diminish the character of the aggressor. Witnesses to the incident will shelter the victim and show nothing but disdain toward the other. At the end of it all, I am still a man passive to my enemies, remembering always that it was never about me.

THE END

www.ingramcontent.com/pod-product-compliance
Lightning Source LLC
Chambersburg PA
CBHW052116030426
42335CB00025B/3004